Understanding and Applying: Mathematical Reasoning, Verbal Reasoning and Language Inference

Sharan Spall

First published in Great Britain in 2020.
Copyright © 2020 Sharan Spall.
It is the right of Sharan Spall to be identified as the author of this work and has been asserted by her in accordance with the Copyright, Designs and Patents Act 1988.
No part of this publication may be reproduced or shared in any form without the prior permission of the author.

Cover image ©

DEDICATION

To all the beautiful children who I have taught, near and far, including my own - Jeevan & Sienna.

"Reasoning and understanding exist not to make simple things complicated, but to make complicated things simple."

WHAT OTHERS SAY

"Sharan Spall has written an outstanding book that covers concepts and questions that are fundamental for students who are preparing for the 11+ exams. What makes this book unique is the fact that it focuses on applying inference and problem-solving skills - two areas that students tend to really struggle with. If you want your child to score top marks and become more familiar with 11+ exam-style questions, I'd wholeheartedly recommend 'Understanding and Applying Mathematical Reasoning, Verbal Reasoning and Language Inference.'"
Victoria Ademosu - Founder, TheTutoress.com.

"With several years' experience of preparing children for the 11+ exams under her belt, Sharan has identified topics which children often find challenging and, subsequently, struggle with. In this book, she provides targeted exercises for these topics along with answers, which will allow parents to support their children's learning at home. This book will equip children with invaluable competence and agility in these subject areas."
Nkem Ivara - English & Verbal Reasoning Tutor and Founder, Wordsmythe Tutoring.

CONTENTS

Introduction from the author — p.7

A guide to the key terms used in the book — p.8

Exercises:

Chapter one

- Mathematical Reasoning: Directed numbers — p.9
- Verbal Reasoning: Using words, symbols and numbers — p.11
- Language Inference: Looking at Tom Sawyer, by Mark Twain — p.13

Chapter two

- Mathematical Reasoning: Highest Common Factor (HCF) — p.17
- Verbal Reasoning: Patterns and sequences — p.20
- Language Inference: Looking at Eye of the Hurricane, by Lee Roddy — p.23

Chapter three

- Mathematical Reasoning: Lowest Common Multiple (LCM) — p.27
- Verbal Reasoning: Decoding word puzzles — p.30
- Language Inference: Looking at Cider with Rosie, by Laurie Lee — p.33

Chapter four

- Mathematical Reasoning: Mean, Median, Mode and Range — p.38
- Verbal Reasoning: Understanding synonyms and word codes — p.41
- Language Inference: Looking at Volcano Adventure, by Willard Price — p.43

Chapter five

- Mathematical Reasoning: **Mixed Operations of +, -, × and ÷** — p.46
- Verbal Reasoning: Hidden words and word pairs — p.49
- Language Inference: Looking at Christy, by Catherine Marshall — p.51

Chapter six

- Mathematical Reasoning: Multiplying and Dividing with Decimals   p.55
- Verbal Reasoning: Logical sequences   p.58
- Language Inference: Looking at Dracula, by Bram Stoker   p.60

Chapter seven

- Mathematical Reasoning: Percentages   p.64
- Verbal Reasoning: Equations with letters and numbers   p.67
- Language Inference: Treasure Island, by Robert Louis Stevenson   p.69

Chapter eight

- Mathematical Reasoning: Perimeter, Area and Volume   p.73
- Verbal Reasoning: Opposites and similarities   p.76
- Language Inference: Looking at a newspaper article   p.79

Chapter nine

- Mathematical Reasoning: Ratios   p.83
- Verbal Reasoning: Number patterns and word pairs   p.86
- Language Inference: A Pattern of Islands by Arthur Grimble   p.89

Chapter ten

- Mathematical Reasoning: Number sequences   p.93
- Verbal Reasoning: Letter patterns and sequences   p.96
- Language Inference: Looking at a short story by Winston Churchill   p.99

Glossary of terms   p.103

Language techniques   p.105

Progress tracker   p.107

Answers   p.111

INTRODUCTION

Over decades of coaching and tutoring hundreds of primary level children, I've found that there are several key attributes that younger children have in spades: aspiration, self-awareness, curiosity, and vulnerability. They truly want to understand and master new skills; they see themselves very clearly; they constantly think of and ask good questions; and they tolerate their own mistakes as they move up the learning curve.

But, time and time again, I have seen children struggle to understand **why** they are doing something. We know that primary teaching should be about exploring, reasoning and challenging thinking, but all too often learning by rote is prioritized above reasoning.

The exercises in this book are designed to help children and parents to see beyond the letters and numbers, and to develop learning with critical thinking and reasoning skills. They emphasise the importance of deeper understanding over the recalling of facts and will help children to engage fully with and enjoy their learning journey.

In the following ten chapters, you will find the culmination of the key reasoning skills required for pupils sitting 11+ secondary selection tests. This includes students seeking entry to grammar schools and independent senior schools at 11+ and 13+.

Each chapter is presented in three sections:

Section A of each chapter gives your child a Mathematical Reasoning toolkit to help develop a well-rounded foundation for primary to secondary transition.

Section B of each chapter gives your child a range of Verbal Reasoning questions, which are common in 11+ entrance tests.

Section C of each chapter includes an extract from a well-known children's book. Read the extract with your child and attempt to answer the questions together to develop your Language Inference skills.

At the end of each chapter, I'll summarise what your child will have learnt and why the exercise is important in their learning journey. Remember to share this information with your child, so that they can chart their progression and understand how the exercises are helping their learning and development.

Check your child's answers with the answers at the back and give your child a score at the end of each chapter. Remember practice makes perfect!

Wishing your child every success,

Sharan

A GUIDE TO THE KEY TERMS IN THIS BOOK

Mathematical Reasoning

Reasoning in Mathematics is the process of applying logical and critical thinking to a problem in order to work out the correct strategy to use (and as importantly, not to use) in reaching a solution.

Fluency in Maths and memorising **key number facts** is essential in Key Stage 1 and Key Stage 2 Mathematics. However, **using and applying these facts** to a range of contexts, and different types of word problems, including the more complex multi-step and two-step word problems is the essence of Key Stage 2 to Key Stage 3 Mathematics. In this book, I will help you understand the importance of Mathematical Reasoning and how to apply reasoning to problems.

Verbal Reasoning

Verbal Reasoning is, by definition, *'understanding and reasoning using concepts framed in words – it aims at evaluating the ability to think constructively rather than just recognise vocabulary'*. Verbal Reasoning is a test of a skill rather than learnt knowledge.

In this book, you will learn how to use Verbal Reasoning to assess a child's critical thinking skills. It will help children to understand and articulate ***why*** they are doing things, improving their understanding and improving their engagement with learning materials.

Language Inference

You practise Language Inference every day. If a toddler tries a new food for the first time and he scrunches up his face, we can infer that the toddler did not like that food. In this book you will be able to practise Language Inference with your child, looking beyond what is stated in the text and finding the ideas to which the author only hints.

This will make your child a more active reader and critical thinker. However, it's important to understand the literal meaning of the text first, before you move on to exploring the inference. The exercises in this book will help you and your child to progress up this learning curve in the right way.

CHAPTER 1

CHAPTER 1, SECTION A – MATHEMATICAL REASONING

Directed Numbers

The following exercises will help you to practise using directed numbers to describe any quantity that can be measured above or below zero. Common examples of directed numbers include temperature and distance (above or below sea level).

A digit without a "+" or a "–" sign in front of it is positive (+). Example: 5°C means +5°C.

Examples:

1. At noon, the temperature was 25°C. At midnight it had fallen by 26°C. What is the temperature at midnight?

   Answer: +25 – 26 = –1

2. In Toronto, the temperature is – 4°C and in London it is 3°C. Find the difference in temperature between Toronto and London.

   (Remember your number line)

   Answer: +3 – (- 4) = 7

Questions

1. Which temperature is higher? Underline the correct answers. [5 marks]

   a. -2°C   or   6°C

   b. 7°C   or   -11°C

   c. -5°C   or   -1°C

   d. 0°C   or   -2°C

   e. -15°C   or   -17°C

2. What is the difference in temperatures below? [5 marks]

   a. -6°C   and   4°C   Answer: _____

b. -11°C   and   -19°C   Answer: _____

c. -7°C   and   -1.5 °C   Answer: _____

d. -99°C   and   99°C   Answer: _____

e. 0°C   and   -17°C   Answer: _____

3. A climber starts at 125m and descends 75m. How far above sea level does he get to? [1 mark]

Answer: _____

4. The temperature in a freezer is -3°C. The door has been accidentally left open and the temperature has risen by 5°C. What is the new temperature? [1 mark]

Answer: _____

5. Find the values below. [3 marks]

a. $7 + (-9) - (+2)$ Answer:_____

b. $-9 + (-5) - (-6)$ Answer:_____

c. $-10 \times (+3)$ Answer:_____

Total: / 15

CHAPTER 1, SECTION B – VERBAL REASONING

The next two exercises will help your child learn to think using **words, symbols** and **numbers**.

Questions

1. Insert a letter. Find the **one** letter that will complete the word in front of the brackets and begin the word after the brackets. **The same letter must fit into both sets of brackets.** Mark this letter in the space provided.

Example.	BLAS (T) REASON	SHOR (T) RIP
a.	SLU (__) ENTLE	BA (__) IRL
b.	BAL (__) INE	BOW (__) AKE
c.	TA (__) AN	DRO (__) INE
d.	BU (__) ES	GRE (__) ELLOW
e.	BEE (__) ICE	COR (__) EW
f.	LEA (__) IRE	SEL (__) AN
g.	STA (__) END	CRA (__) LOW
h.	SLO (__) ON	DRA (__) EST
i.	COP (__) AWN	TRA (__) OUR
j.	DOO (__) OSE	BEA (__) OOM
k.	GIR (__) OVE	CRAW (__) OSE
l.	CLU (__) AKE	CU (__) ROWN

Total: / 12

2. Number relationship. The numbers in each group are **related** in the same way. Find the missing number in the third group and write it in the space provided.

Example.	(2 [12] 6)	(5 [20] 4)	(3 [27] 9)
a.	(10 [23] 3)	(5 [16] 6)	(2 [__] 5)
b.	(4 [12] 2)	(10 [32] 6)	(16 [__] 5)
c.	(6 [46] 20)	(2 [32] 15)	(7 [__] 10)
d.	(12 [16] 8)	(6 [22] 20)	(15 [__] 13)
e.	(16 [40] 8)	(11 [27] 5)	(4 [__] 11)
f.	(10 [21] 5)	(4 [23] 13)	(21 [__] 9)
g.	(6 [10] 14)	(3 [19] 20)	(4 [__] 9)
h.	(4 [27] 6)	(5 [53] 10)	(8 [__] 2)
i.	(6 [7] 10)	(20 [25] 14)	(11 [__] 8)
j.	(4 [8] 6)	(11 [33] 9)	(6 [__] 12)
k.	(2 [16] 6)	(7 [23] 10)	(2 [__] 4)
l.	(4 [9] 5)	(6 [9] 3)	(7 [__] 4)

Total: ___ / 12

CHAPTER 1, SECTION C – LANGUAGE INFERENCE

The following extract is taken from the novel, <u>Tom Sawyer,</u> by Mark Twain. By applying language inference to this extract, you will able to better understand the context and meaning of the text.

"TOM!"
No answer.
"TOM!"
No answer.
"What's gone with that boy, I wonder? You TOM!"
No answer.

The old lady pulled her spectacles down and looked over them about the room; then she put them up and looked out under them. She seldom or never looked through them for so small a thing as a boy; they were her state pair, the pride of her heart, and were built for "style", not service - she could have seen through a pair of stove-lids just as well. She looked perplexed for a moment, and then said, not fiercely, but still loud enough for the furniture to hear:

"Well, I lay if I get hold of you, I'll…"

She did not finish, for by this time she was bending down and punching under the bed with the broom, and so she needed breath to punctuate the punches with. She resurrected nothing but the cat.

"I never did see the beat of that boy!"

She went to the open door and stood in it and looked out among the tomato vines and "jimpson" weeds that constituted the garden. No Tom. She lifted her voice at an angle calculated for distance and shouted:

"Y-o-u-u Tom!"

There was a slight noise behind her, and she turned just in time to seize a small boy by the slack of his dungarees and arrest his flight.

"There! I might 'a' thought of that closet. What you been doing in there?"
"Nothing."
"Nothing! Look at your hands. And look at your mouth. What is that truck?"
"I don't know, aunt."
"Well, I know. It is jam! – that's what it is. Forty times I've said if you didn't let that jam alone, I'd skin you. Hand me that switch."

The switch hovered in the air - the peril was desperate – "My! Look behind you, aunt!"

The old lady whirled round and snatched her skirts out of danger. The lad fled on the instant, scrambled up the high board-fence, and disappeared over it. His aunt Polly stood surprised a moment, and then broke into a gentle laugh.

"Hang the boy, can't I never learn anything? Ain't he played me tricks enough like that for me to be looking out for him by this time? But old fools is the biggest fools there is. Can't teach an old dog new tricks, as the saying is.

Questions

Answer in full sentences and in your own words as far as possible:

1. Why is the word 'TOM!' written in capital letters in the first line? [1 mark]

Answer:_____

2. What does the expression "The pride of her heart" mean? [1 mark]

Answer:_____

3. "The old lady's spectacles were built for "style", not service." What does this mean? [2 marks]

Answer:_____

_____

4. Why does the old lady punch under the bed with the broom? [1 mark]

Answer:_____

5. How do we know that the old lady is unsuccessful when she punches under the bed with a broom? [1 mark]

Answer:_____

6. What does "resurrected" mean? [1 mark]

Answer:_____

7. Where had the boy been hiding? [1 mark]

Answer:_____

8. Why had the boy been hiding? [1 mark]

Answer:_____

9. What do you think a "switch" is? [1 mark]

Answer:_____

10. Explain what the phrase "the peril was desperate" means. [1 mark]

Answer:_____

11. How does the boy escape from his aunt? [1 mark]

Answer:_____

12. How does the boy's aunt react when he escapes? [1 mark]

Answer:_____

13. How do we know that the boy has done this sort of thing before? [1 mark]

Answer:_____

14. "Can't teach an old dog new tricks.." What does this saying mean? [1 mark]

Answer:_____

15. The aunt uses interesting expressions in her speech. Rewrite these sayings in correct English. [3 marks]

a. "I never did see the beat of that boy!"

Answer:_____

b. "What *is* that truck?"

Answer:_____

c. "Forty times I've said if you didn't let that jam alone I'd skin you."

Answer:_____

16. "Y-o-u-u Tom!" What does the punctuation in this sentence tell us about the way the old lady says this? [1 mark]

Answer:_____

Total: / 19

My Chapter 1 Score: / 58 = _____ %

Well done! In chapter one you have learnt that directed numbers are either positive or negative. By completing the exercises in chapter one, you have begun to apply reasoning skills and inference to your Maths and English work. You will now start to understand the 'why' of Mathematical problems, applying logical and critical thinking to the work you're doing. And, by applying language inference to literary excerpts, you will be able to better understand the context and meaning of the text.

CHAPTER 2

CHAPTER 2, SECTION A – MATHEMATICAL REASONING

Highest Common Factor

In this exercise you will learn how to use **prime numbers** and **prime factors**, as well as applying prime factorisation to problems.

Prime Number

A Prime Number is a whole number that cannot be made by multiplying two whole numbers. If we can make it by multiplying two whole numbers, it is a Composite Number. 1 is not prime and not composite.

Prime Factor

A Prime Factor is a factor that is a prime number. In other words: If any prime numbers can be multiplied to give the original number then we say that this number is a prime factor. Example: The prime factors of 15 are 3 and 5 (because $3 \times 5 = 15$, and 3 and 5 are prime numbers).

Prime Factorisation

Prime factorisation is finding which prime numbers multiply together to make the original number.

Highest Common Factor

A Factor is a number that divides into another number exactly (i.e. no remainder). Example: 6 is a factor of 36, but 6 is NOT a factor of 37.

When looking at 2 or more numbers, they may all have a common factor, but the Highest Common Factor (HCF) is the largest of these common factors.

Example:

Find the HCF of 12, 16 and 40

First express each number using Prime Factors.

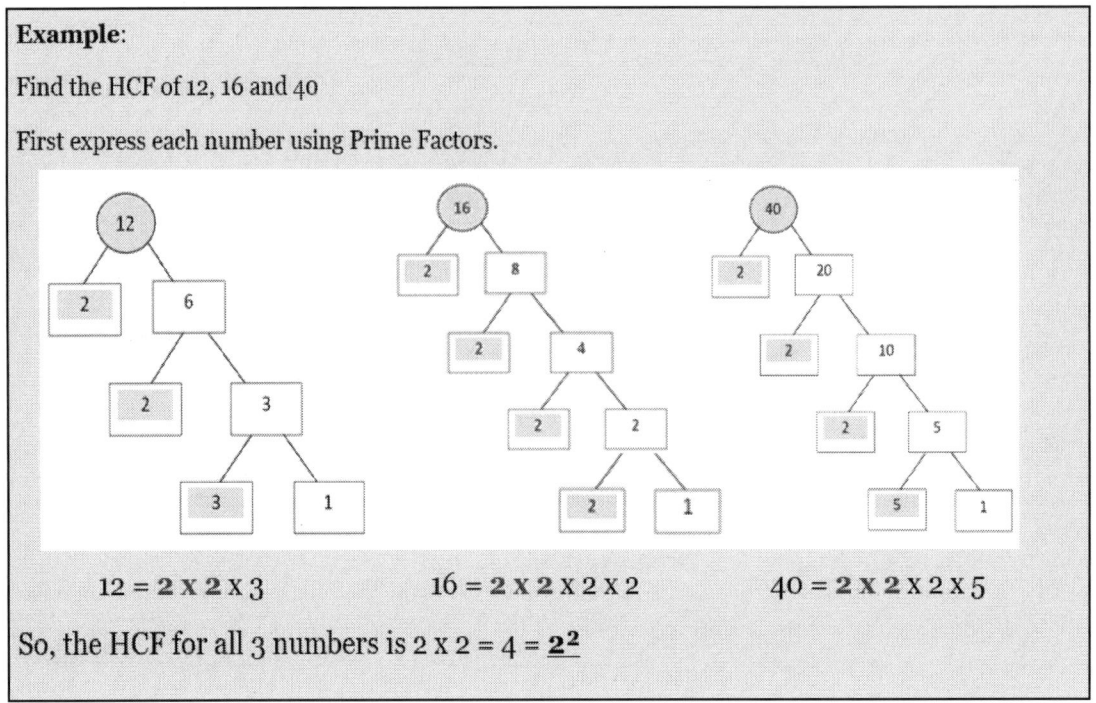

$12 = 2 \times 2 \times 3$ $\qquad$ $16 = 2 \times 2 \times 2 \times 2$ $\qquad$ $40 = 2 \times 2 \times 2 \times 5$

So, the HCF for all 3 numbers is $2 \times 2 = 4 = \underline{\mathbf{2^2}}$

Questions

1. In the list of numbers below, work out which ones have 6 as a factor. [1 mark]

    16 , 26 , 24 , 52 , 46 , 48 , 36 , 76

Answer: _____

2. List all the prime numbers between 50 and 70. [1 mark]

Answer: _____

3. Find the prime factors of 360. [2 marks]

Answer: _____

4. Find the prime factors of 1250. [2 marks]

Answer: _____

5. Find the Common Prime Factors of 15, 60 and 85. [5 marks]

Answer: _____

6. Find the HCF of the following using prime factors and powers. [1 mark]

   $2 \times 2 \times 2 \times 5 \times 5$

   $2 \times 2 \times 3 \times 7$

   $2 \times 2 \times 2 \times 5 \times 11$

Answer: _____

7. Find the HCFs. [3 marks]

   a. 48 , 80 and 112

Answer: _____

   b. 90 , 198 and 234

Answer: _____

   d. 324 , 432 and 560

Answer: _____

Total: / 15

CHAPTER 2, SECTION B – VERBAL REASONING

The next exercise will help you to spot words which do not belong in a list, and will interrogate your critical thinking as we ask you **why** the words you've chosen don't fit into the list. The second task will help you learn to think about **patterns** and **sequences** using the letters in the alphabet.

Questions

1. Find the odd words. Find the **two** words that are **different** from the other three and write them in the space provided. Give a brief reason for your answers.

Example.	Monday Tuesday Friday month noon <u>month</u> and <u>noon</u> My reason why: *Monday, Tuesday* and *Friday* are days of the week, whereas *month* and *noon* are not.
a.	cat horse duck chicken dog _____ and _____ My reason why:
b.	planet Venus Earth Mars space _____ and _____ My reason why:
c.	cooker boil roast eat fry _____ and _____ My reason why:
d.	swimming judo cricket rugby football _____ and _____ My reason why:
e.	lamb horse pig calf foal _____ and _____ My reason why:

f.	mother father daughter nephew sister _____ and _____ My reason why:	
g.	unusual unwell untied ill sick _____ and _____ My reason why:	
h.	knife plate cup spoon saucer _____ and _____ My reason why:	
i.	carrot strawberry pear bean lettuce _____ and _____ My reason why:	
j.	uncle actress boy girl master _____ and _____ My reason why:	
k.	pair orange banana couple duo _____ and _____ My reason why:	
l.	mower grass trimmer bush plant _____ and _____ My reason why:	

Total: / 12

2. Alphabet series. Find the pair of letters that continue each **series** in the most sensible way. Write the answer in the space provided.

A B C D E F G H I J K L M N O P Q R S T U V W X Y Z

Example.	AB, BC, CD, DE, EF,	(<u>FG</u>	)
a.	AJ, BI, CH, DG, EF,	(	)
b.	NK, PM, RO, TQ, VS,	(	)
c.	QR, PP, ON, NL, MJ,	(	)
d.	CZ, BY, AX, ZW, YV,	(	)
e.	KL, LM, MN, NO, OP,	(	)
f.	RH, PJ, NL, LN, JP,	(	)
g.	AB, EF, IJ, MN, QR,	(	)
h.	US, VT, WU, XV, YW,	(	)
i.	GB, FD, EF, DH, CJ,	(	)
j.	RR, NP, JN, FL, BJ,	(	)
k.	RG, SH, UJ, XM, BQ,	(	)
l.	QM, OO, MQ, KS, IU,	(	)

Total: / 12

CHAPTER 2, SECTION C – LANGUAGE INFERENCE

The following extract is taken from the novel, <u>Eye of the Hurricane</u>, by Lee Roddy. By applying language inference to this extract, you will better understand the context and meaning of the text.

MIGHTY gusts of wind continued to shake the swamp shack where another violent gust of wind tore at the loosened corner of the roof.

"There it goes!" Tank exclaimed as the corner started to sag under the weight of rain.

A piece of corrugated sheeting sailed away, and the corner collapsed inward, causing everyone to scramble up and back as far away as possible.

"We're dead!" Garcia screamed. "We're all dead!"

"No, we're not!" the pilot cried. "The weight of the water on the roof caused that corner to collapse, but it'll soon drain off. Besides, I think I hear the storm easing off. So if that end of the roof holds up a little while longer, we can start for the cave."

Everyone except Garcia fell silent. He sank back down against the wall, closed his eyes and mumbled over and over, "Oh, God! Oh, God!"

It took a moment for Josh to realise that the man was praying in the only way he knew how.

Josh joined the others in listening hopefully as the rain and wind slowly faded away. Falling rain from the collapsed end of the roof eased off too, but there was so much water on the floor that everyone's feet were wet.

Finally, Eddie stood up. "The eye of the hurricane is almost here," he announced. "We'll have about fifteen minutes to reach the cave before the back side of the storm starts..."

"I'm getting out of here now!" Frank interrupted, hoisting himself to his feet and pulling on his raincoat. "Come on, Garcia. If you want to live through this thing, you've got to help yourself."

"Wait!" the pilot cried, but the big poacher yanked the door open and plunged through it.

The wind and rain gushed into the tiny room, making it rock so hard Josh feared it would blow off the foundation. The force of the wind made him turn his head momentarily. When he looked again, Frank and Garcia were gone, leaving their backpacks behind.

Eddie said sadly, "They shouldn't have done that."

A few minutes later, Eddie decided it was safe to head for the cave. Everyone stood and stepped outside.

Now only light rain fell, unlike the blinding downpour of the past few hours. The incredible gusting winds had completely died down. Josh squinted at the sky. The dark clouds warned that this was only a momentary lull. Greater natural fury was coming.

"Fifteen minutes before the eye passes," Eddie warned. "We'd better be in the cave before then, or we may not be so lucky when the back side of the storm hits."

It was very hard going because the hillside was slick, and there were countless downed trees, uprooted shrubs and mud slides everywhere. Still, Josh was so glad to be out of the shack that he didn't really mind.

Maybe Dad and Dr Nakamura are in the cave, Josh thought, ignoring the mud that weighted down his shoes. He hurried through the hurricane's eye in renewed hope.

Questions

Answer full sentences and in your own words as far as possible:

1. What is a shack? [1 mark]

   Answer:_____

2. "There it goes!" To what is Tank referring? [1 mark]

   Answer:_____

3. Why was it important to change locations only during the eye of the hurricane? [1 mark]

   Answer:_____

4. Find a word in the passage that tells us what Frank's occupation is. Explain what this means in your own words. [2 marks]

   Answer:_____

5. What is a "momentary lull"? [1 mark]

   Answer:_____

6. "Greater natural fury was coming." What does this mean? [2 marks]

   Answer:_____

7. In your own words, why did the group find it difficult to climb up the hillside? [3 marks]

Answer:_____

_____

_____

8. Why do you think Josh had "renewed hope"? [1 mark]

Answer:_____

9. Underline the correct answer. "The hillside was "slick"". What does this word mean? [1 mark]

    a. wet

    b. slippery

    c. unwell

    d. steep

10. Write the meaning of the following words as they are used in the passage. [4 marks]

    a. mumble_____

    b. downed_____

    c. foundation_____

    d. fury_____

11. For each of the following words, write down a word that is opposite in meaning. [4 marks]

   a. mighty _____

   b. continued _____

   c. hopefully _____

   d. gushed _____

Total: / 21

My Chapter 2 Score: / 60 = _____ %

Congratulations on completing chapter two. You're now developing your mathematical skills particularly by combining your knowledge of factors, multiples and prime numbers. You have been introduced to Prime Factorisation as a means of finding the Highest Common Factor. Lots of children confuse these terms but by completing these exercises you are beginning to strengthen your mathematical-muscle. Well done! You have also been introduced to grouping nouns to find the odd ones out – and by reading Eye of the Hurricane you have gone on to infer the meaning of the extract and explore the language that has been used.

CHAPTER 3

CHAPTER 3, SECTION A – MATHEMATICAL REASONING

Lowest Common Multiple

A **multiple** is a number which can be divided by another number without leaving a remainder.

Example: 15 is a multiple of 3, but 16 is not a multiple of 3.

Sometimes you will need to find the **Lowest Common Multiple (LCM)** to help solve a problem. The LCM of 2 or more numbers is the smallest number than can be divided by them without leaving a remainder. This exercise will help you to use the LCMs in Mathematical problems.

Examples:

1. Find the LCM of 12, 16 and 40.

   First express each number using **Prime Factors.**
   $12 = 2 \times 2 \times 3$
   $16 = 2 \times 2 \times 2 \times 2$
   $40 = 2 \times 2 \times 2 \times 5$

   The LCM of these numbers **must** have the factors listed above.
   Remember you only list them out once.
   Answer: $2 \times 2 \times 2 \times 2 \times 3 \times 5 =$ **240**

2. Find the LCM of 180 and 252 using prime factors and powers.

   $180 = 2 \times 2 \times 3 \times 3 \times 5$
   $252 = 2 \times 2 \times 3 \times 3 \times 7$

   The LCM of these numbers is $2 \times 2 \times 3 \times 3 \times 5 \times 7$
   Answer: **$2^2 \times 3^2 \times 5 \times 7$**

Questions

1. Find the LCM of the following. [6 marks]

   a. 4 and 6

   Answer:_____

b. 9 and 12

Answer:_____

c. 10, 16 and 18

Answer:_____

d. 24, 32 and 40

Answer:_____

e. 30, 45, 75 and 95

Answer:_____

f. 80, 70, 110 and 150

Answer:_____

2. A small amount of powder can be divided into equal heaps of 6g, 8g or 12g. Find the smallest amount of powder for which this would be possible. [1 mark]

Answer:_____

3. Find the smallest sum of money that is an EXACT multiple of 60p, 72p and £1.12. [1 mark]

Answer:_____

4. Find the smallest number of marbles that could be shared equally into bags of 15, 20 or 24 marbles. [1 mark]

Answer:_____

5. In a local church the bells are rung at regular intervals of 4s, 6s and 9s. If they begin ringing at the same time, how long will it be before they ring at the same time again? [1mark]

Answer:_____

Total: / 10

CHAPTER 3, SECTION B – VERBAL REASONING

By **decoding** these puzzles, you will be able to find meaning in seemingly random groups of letters.

Questions

1. The first code word in each question has been worked out for you. Work out the second word / code in the question in the same way and write it in the space provided.

A B C D E F G H I J K L M N O P Q R S T U V W X Y Z

Example.	If the code for TRAP is USBQ What does DPME mean?	(	**COLD**	)
a.	If the code for BALL is CBMM What does UPZT mean?	(		)
b.	If GHOC means FIND What does MNTS mean?	(		)
c.	If the code for JUMP is LWOR What is the code for SPIN?	(		)
d.	If the code for DOWN is BMUL What does MTCP mean?	(		)
e.	If IDCS means LEFT What is the code for HALF?	(		)
f.	If the code for MISS is NLTV What is the code for ACHE?	(		)
g.	If VTCA means TRAY What does IKXG mean?	(		)
h.	If the code for FOWL is GQZP What is the code for SLIP?	(		)
i.	If the code for NAIL is REMP What does XIWX mean?	(		)

j.	IF GEEL means EACH What does PSPI mean?	( )
k.	If RRLL means STOP What is the code for GONE?	( )
l.	If the code for STAB is TSCZ What is the code for PLUS?	( )

Total: / 12

2. Find the two words, one from each group that will complete the sentence in the best way. Underline **BOTH** words below.

Example.	Time is to (first, **second**, third) as distance is to (gram, kilo, **metre**).
a.	Top is to (lid, bottom, win) as inside is to (outside, closed, trapped).
b.	Grass is to (long, green, tall) as corn is to (flour, flake, yellow).
c.	Cow is to (field, bull, herd) as sheep is to (flock, wool, lamb).
d.	Sum is to (add, some, total) as sun is to (moon, stars, son).
e.	Octagon is to (six, seven, eight) as pentagon is to (four, five, six).
f.	Cheap is to (bird, expect, expensive) as always is to (sometimes, often, never).
g.	Clean is to (wash, sparkle, dirty) as brush is to (dust, sweep, scrape).
h.	Divide is to (change, remainder, multiply) as add is to (subtract, equals, plus).

i.	Hand is to (mouth, arm, glove) as foot is to (toes, sock, ball).
j.	Sea is to (beach, see, shore) as tide is to (waves, tied, water).
k.	Banana is to (fruit, custard, curved) as onion is to (cry, ring, vegetable).
l.	Light is to (sun, bulb, heavy) as tight is to (mean, loose, close).

Total: / 12

CHAPTER 3, SECTION C – LANGUAGE INFERENCE

The following extract is taken from, Cider with Rosie, by Laurie Lee. It is about a little boy's first day at school. By applying language inference to this extract, you will be able to better understand the context and meaning of the text.

THE village school at that time provided all the instruction we were likely to ask for. It was a small stone barn divided by a wooden partition into two rooms - The Infants and The Big Ones. There was one dame teacher and perhaps a young girl assistant. Every child in the valley went there, remained till he was fourteen years old, then was presented to the working field or factory with nothing in his head but a few sayings, a jumbled list of wars, and a dreamy image of the world's geography. It seemed enough to get by with, in any case; and was one up on our poor old grandparents.

This school, when I came to it, was at its peak. It was packed to the walls with pupils. Wild boys and girls from miles around - from the outlying farms and half-hidden hovels way up at the ends of the valley - swept down each day to add to our numbers, bringing with them strange oaths and odours, quaint garments and curious pies. They were my first amazed vision of any world outside the womanly warmth of my family; I didn't expect to survive it for long, and I was confronted with it at the age of four.

The morning came, without any warning, when my sisters surrounded me, wrapped me in scarves, tied up my bootlaces, thrust a cap on my head and stuffed a baked potato in my pocket.

"What's this?" I asked.
"You're starting school today."
"I ain't. I'm stopping 'ome."
"Now, come on, Loll. You're a big boy now."
"I ain't."
"You are."
"Boo-hoo."

They picked me up bodily, kicking and bawling, and carried me up the road.

"Boys who don't go to school get put in boxes, and turn into rabbits, and get chopped up on Sundays."

I felt this was overdoing it rather, but I said no more after that. I arrived at the school just three feet tall and fatly wrapped in my scarves. The playground roared like a rodeo, and the potato burned through my thigh. Old boots, ragged stockings, torn trousers and skirts, went skidding and skating around me. The rabble closed in; I was encircled, grit flew in my face like shrapnel. Tall girls with frizzled hair, and huge boys with sharp elbows, began to prod me with hideous interest. They plucked at my scarves, spun me around like a top, twisted my nose, and stole my potato.

I was rescued at last by a gracious lady - the sixteen-year-old junior-teacher - who boxed a few ears and dried my face and led me off to The Infants. I spent that first day picking holes in paper, then went home in a smouldering temper.

"What's the matter, Loll? Didn't he like it at school, then?"
"They never gave me the present!"
"Present? What present?"
"They said they'd give me a present."
"Well, now, I'm sure they didn't."
"They did! They said: 'You're Laurie Lee, ain't you? Well, you just sit there for the present."
"I sat there all day but I never got it. I ain't going back there again!"

But after a week I felt like a veteran and grew as ruthless as anyone else. Somebody had stolen my baked potato, so I swiped somebody else's apple.

Questions

1. Underline the correct answer. The narrator says that his education was "one up on our poor old grandparents." This phrase means? [1 mark]

    a. It was a better education than his grandparents had had.

    b. It was a worse education than his grandparents had had.

    c. His own grandparents had been too poor to go to school.

    d. His grandparents went to school for a very long time.

2. In your own words, say what the four things were that the wild boys and girls brought to school with them. [4 marks]

Answer:_____

_____

_____

3. In the third paragraph, what tells us that the narrator's family suspected that he would not want to go to school? [1 mark]

Answer:_____

4. "I ain't. I'm stopping 'ome." Rewrite this in correct English. [1 mark]

Answer:_____

5. a. What does Laurie do to try and stop them from sending him to school? [1 mark]

Answer:_____

   b. What eventually convinces Laurie to go to school? [2 marks]

Answer:_____

_____

6. a. Underline what figure of speech this is: [1 mark]

"The playground roared like a rodeo."

    i. metaphor

    ii. simile

    iii. alliteration

6. b. Do you think the figure of speech is effective? Why? [1 mark]

Answer:_____

7. Underline the correct answer. The pupils show "hideous interest" in Laurie. This means? [1 mark]

    a. They were ugly but interesting.

    b. They were interested in how ugly Laurie was.

    c. Laurie did not like the way they showed their interest in him.

    d. Laurie found them interesting but ugly.

8. The teacher told Laurie to "sit there for the present".

   a. What did the teacher mean? [1 mark]

Answer:_____

   b. What did Laurie think the teacher meant? [1 mark]

Answer:_____

9. How do we know that Laurie did not take long to settle into school life? [1 mark]

Answer:_____

10. In the paragraph which describes the playground, find a word that means: "small pieces of metal from an exploding bomb or grenade." [1 mark]

Answer:_____

11. Write the meaning of the following words as they are used in the passage. [3 marks]

   a. jumbled _____

   b. hovels _____

   c. gracious _____

Total: / 20

My Chapter 3 Score: / 54 = _____ %

Well done for completing chapter three. In this chapter you have used your mathematical reasoning skills to find the Lowest Common Multiple by using prime factors. You've also used your decoding skills to find meaning in letters, a tricky skill to master but one which will be particularly useful as you transition from primary to secondary education. Once again, you're mastering your language inference skills, looking deeper at text to explore the meaning and context of the piece.

CHAPTER 4

CHAPTER 4, SECTION A – MATHEMATICAL REASONING

Mean, Median, Mode and Range

When working with data, it can be useful to represent the entire data set with a single value that describes the "middle" or "average" value of the entire set. In statistics, that single value is called the central tendency and mean, median and mode are all ways to describe it.

Median is the middle number when all of the numbers are arranged from smallest to largest.
Mean is the total of all the numbers divided by the number of items.
Mode is the number that is the most common.
Range is the difference between the highest and lowest numbers.

Examples:

1. Using the numbers below, find the Mean, Median, Mode and Range.

    5, 3, 7, 9, 5, 2, 1, 3, 5

    Mean = Total ÷ Number

    $= (5 + 3 + 9 + 12 + 5 + 2 + 1 + 3 + 5) \div 9 = 45 \div 9 = \underline{5}$

    Median

    - First arrange the numbers from smallest to largest: 1 2 3 3 5 5 5 7 9
    - Then find the middle number: 1 2 3 3 **5** 5 5 7 9

    Mode

    - The most common number is **5**

    Range = Highest value – Lowest value = 9 – 1 = **8**

Questions

1. For each of the lists below, find the mean, median, mode and range. [5 marks]

    a. 2, 2, 5, 7, 9

    Answers: Mean =   Median =   Mode =   Range =

    b. 4, 5, 8, 8, 10, 11, 17

    Answers: Mean =   Median =   Mode =   Range =

c. 10, 13, 13, 16, 16, 16, 21

Answers: Mean =	Median =	Mode =	Range =

d. 25, 27, 28, 29, 29, 29, 32, 35, 36

Answers: Mean =	Median =	Mode =	Range =

e. 37, 38, 35, 42, 35, 37, 35

Answers: Mean =	Median =	Mode =	Range =

2. A DIY supplier states that on average each box contains 25 matches. In a DIY store the shopkeeper checks a few boxes to see if this is true. Listed below is the number of matches he found in the boxes he checked.

25 , 20 , 35 , 27 , 26 , 24 , 32 , 26 , 28

Work out the mean number of matches in the boxes that he checked. [1 mark]

Answer: _____

3. My mum went shopping and bought lots of potatoes. I took some out and weighed them. Listed below is the weight of each potato.

100g , 85g , 95g , 100g , 96g [3 marks]

   a. Work out the median weight.

Answer: _____

   b. Work out the mean weight.

Answer: _____

   c. What is the range?

Answer: _____

4. The heights of some children in a Year 7 class were noted down.

160cm, 152cm, 155cm, 145cm, 156cm, 166cm, 145cm, 160cm, 159cm, 149cm, 166cm, 160cm, 159cm, 143cm, 150cm, 151cm [2 marks]

   a. Work out the median height.

Answer: _____

   b. What is the range of heights?

Answer: _____

5. Four numbers have a mean of 2. I add on another number and the mean changes to 4. Work out the number that I added. [1 mark]

Answer: _____

6. 5 numbers have a mean of 20. I add on another number and the mean changes to 24. Work out the number that I added. [1 mark]

Answer: _____

Total: / 13

CHAPTER 4, SECTION B – VERBAL REASONING

Synonyms

The use of **synonyms** helps to make your writing more vivid and to create a more intriguing image in the mind of the reader.

Questions

1. Find two words, **one from each group**, that are the **closest in meaning** and underline them.

Example.	(<u>sleep</u> run walk)	(smile laugh <u>snooze</u>)
a.	(many few some)	(type kind lots)
b.	(bead mine beat)	(hit use gold)
c.	(ask speak laugh)	(try talk forget)
d.	(money pay cheque)	(cash shopping check)
e.	(push jump slip)	(ice slide walk)
f.	(seaside holiday rock)	(spade stone sand)
g.	(jump bounce trip)	(leap slide swing)
h.	(plate cup saucer)	(tumbler face mug)
i.	(borrow fork spade)	(shovel bucket pail)
j.	(push pull stretch)	(shave shift shove)
k.	(table chair bed)	(sink stool chest)
l.	(loop polo pool)	(river stream pond)

Total: / 12

2. You are given <u>four words</u> and <u>three codes</u>. The words and codes are not in any particular order. Each of the codes matches one of the words. One word has no code. Find a code for a given word or find a word from a given code.

FAR	**ARE**	**EAT**	**OAK**
	963	679	167

a. Find the code for the word TEAR. (_____)

b. Find the code for the word FATE. (_____)

c. Find the word for the code 7639. (_____)

MILE	**SLIM**	**MEAN**	**LIME**
	6738	3845	3768

d. Find the code for the word LINEN. (_____)

e. Find the code for the word MALE. (_____)

f. Find the word for the code 6845. (_____)

SEAL	**LEAF**	**FOIL**	**LOAF**
	8754	4768	1264

g. Find the code for the word FLIES. (_____)

h. Find the code for the word LOSE. (_____)

i. Find the word for the code 84261. (_____)

Total: / 9

CHAPTER 4, SECTION C – LANGUAGE INFERENCE

The following extract is taken from a novel entitled <u>Volcano Adventure</u>, by Willard Price. By applying language inference to this extract, you will be able to better understand the context and meaning of the text.

THE darkness was turning from black to grey. Day was coming. Presently there was enough light to see by and they could turn off their torches.

And what a dreary waste they saw! Great black blocks of lava, streams of ashes, not a tree, not a bush, not a blade of grass. The moon itself could not be any more bare and bald. This was a place where nothing dared to grow and it seemed as if man himself had no right to be here.

Only the fog was perfectly at home, rushing and rippling over the wet black rocks. It came in bursts and billows. One moment you could see twenty feet ahead, the next moment you could hardly see your hand before your face.

In the darkness and fog they had lost what little trail there had been. Now they simply blundered upward, slipping in the ashes, scratched by the sharp, glossy ridges of lava, clambering up cliffs like mountain goats, trying to keep their balance when the ground shook. Suddenly a violent quake made the rocks bounce. There was a sliding, ripping sound above them.

"Look out!" cried the doctor, "Under this ledge - quick!"

The six huddled in the shallow cave under the projecting ledge as tons of rock, ash and cinder thundered down like a deadly waterfall within a few feet of their faces. While it passed their hiding place it completely blocked out the light. Then it rampaged down the mountainside, its roar becoming fainter and fainter as it was swallowed up in the fog.

At last the ground began to level out and the six weary vulcanologists found themselves upon what appeared to be the top of the mountain. But where was the crater?

This was no simple volcano. It did not rise to a point. The top of the mountain consisted of mile upon mile of hilly country. Somewhere there was a crater. But, without a trail to follow, who could tell where it might be? In clear weather the rising smoke could be seen. In this dense fog, the six explorers could only see each other. As the group marched on, the roar of the volcano grew louder. The sun had risen but was unable to get through the fog.
The fog was more dense than ever because evil gasses and smoke had joined it.

But in spite of the fumes and falling stones and the quaking of the ground and the increasing thunder of the monster, Dr Dan strode along boldly, almost too boldly - as if he were afraid to show fear. Suddenly he came to an abrupt halt.

"We have arrived!" he cried.

The others came up beside him. A few feet ahead the ground dropped away to nothing. Great billows of smoke rose to mingle with the flying fog.

Their eyes could make out nothing but their ears told them that they were standing at the edge of the crater. A noise like the roar of ten thousand angry lions came up from the pit.

Beneath that noise there was another like the rumble of freight trains over a bridge. Then there was a higher note, the sound of escaping steam, like the hiss of a great serpent. And there were sudden explosions as if charges of dynamite were being set off. The noise was ear-splitting.

Questions

1. Why was it a "place where nothing dared to grow"? [1 mark]

Answer:_____

2. "Rock, ash and cinder thundered down like a deadly waterfall". What figure of speech is this and why is it a good comparison? [2 marks]

Answer:_____

_____

3. What do you think a vulcanologist is? [1 mark]

Answer:_____

4. a. Why did the weather hinder their search for the crater? [1 mark]

Answer:_____

b. Why would clear weather be better? [1 mark]

Answer:_____

5. In your own words, say why it was "no simple volcano". [1 mark]

Answer:_____

6. What helped to make the fog so dense? [1 mark]

Answer:_____

7. In your own words, say why Dr Dan "strode along boldly". [1 mark]

Answer:_____

8. "The noise was ear-splitting." What does this mean? [1 mark]

Answer:_____

9. Write the meaning of the following words as they are used in the passage. [5 marks]

    a. dreary_____

    b. glossy _____

    c. weary _____

    d. abrupt _____

    e. freight _____

Total: / 15

My Chapter 4 Score: / 49 = _____ %

Well done on completing another chapter successfully. Learning about median, mode and range will help you to better understand data sets, particularly large amounts of data. Your work on synonyms in this chapter will not only help with your comprehension of literary text, but will also help to make your own writing more vivid and engaging. Really useful!

CHAPTER 5

CHAPTER 5, SECTION A – MATHEMATICAL REASONING

Mixed Operations of +, -, × and ÷

Operations mean things like add, subtract, multiply, divide, squaring, etc. If it isn't a number it is probably an operation. But, when you see something like...

$$7 + (6 \times 5^2 + 3)$$

... what part should you calculate first?
Start at the left and go to the right?
Or go from right to left?

Warning: Calculate them in the wrong order, and you can get a wrong answer!

The **order** of mathematical operations can be remembered by using BIDMAS.

B = Brackets
I = Indices / Other
D = Division
M = Multiplication
A = Addition
S = Subtraction

Example:
1. What is $(5 \times 10) + 10 \div 2 - 6$?

    Work out the brackets first: $(5 \times 10) = 50$

    Then divide: $10 \div 2 = 5$

    Then add: $50 + 5 = 55$

    Finally subtract: $55 - 6 = \underline{\mathbf{49}}$

Questions

1. $(3 \times 6) \div 2$

Answer: _____

2. $9 - (8 \div 4) \times 2$

Answer: _____

Understanding and Applying: Mathematical Reasoning, Verbal Reasoning and Language Inference

3. $19 \times 7 + 3 - 6$

Answer: _____

4. $4 \times 3 \div 3 + 20$

Answer: _____

5. $25 \div 5 + 6$

Answer: _____

6. $4 + 3 \times (2 - 1) + 10 \div (15 - 13)$

Answer: _____

7. $3 + 3 \times 3 - 3 + 3$

Answer: _____

8. $3 \times (8 - 2) + 5 \times (8 - 4)$

Answer: _____

9. $7 + 3 \times (9 - 5) + 25 \div (18 - 13)$

Answer: _____

10. $(54 \div 6)^2 \times (13 - 7)$

Answer: _____

11. $(35 \div 7 + 3) + (9 \times 9 - 79)$

Answer: _____

12. $(60 \div 5 + 7) - (7 \times 3 + 3)$

Answer: _____

13. $8^2 \div 2 \times 10$

Answer: _____

14. $(17 - 10 \div 2) \div (8 \div 2 - 2)$

Answer: _____

15. $(7 - 9 + 10) \times (144 \div 12 - 12)$

Answer: _____

Total: /15

CHAPTER 5, SECTION B – VERBAL REASONING

By finding the hidden word in a sentence and completing word pairs, you'll look closer at words and practise your decoding skills

Questions

1. A **four-letter** word is hidden at the end of one word and the beginning of the next word. Find the pair of words that contain the hidden word. Write the new word in the space provided.

Example.	The probe streaked through outer space.	(<u>best</u>)
a.	Three envelopes had some cash inside.	( )
b.	My dogs eat lots of food.	( )
c.	Monday was pleasant and sunny.	( )
d.	Buses often run on busy roads.	( )
e.	People don't drive fast on the motorway.	( )
f.	The packet has one crisp inside.	( )
g.	Cats are less friendly than dogs.	( )
h.	The pope arrived at the airport.	( )
i.	Fred owned lots of china animals.	( )
j.	Sandra has suffered from a few illnesses.	( )
k.	Grandma steered the boat towards Dover.	( )
l.	Some boys have stolen my bicycle.	( )

Total / 12

Understanding and Applying: Mathematical Reasoning, Verbal Reasoning and Language Inference

2. In these questions there are three pairs of words. Complete the third pair in the same way as the first two pairs. Write the new word in the space provided.

Example.	(grind, grin)	(fore, for)	(piper, **pipe**)
a.	(vile, evil)	(reef, free)	(ours, _____)
b.	(keep, peek)	(deal, lead)	(dear, _____)
c.	(trap, part)	(pans, snap)	(flog, _____)
d.	(sick, tick)	(book, cook)	(last, _____)
e.	(sneers, see)	(gained, din)	(crater, _____)
f.	(photos, shop)	(priced, drip)	(pliers, _____)
g.	(roar, oar)	(doll, old)	(team, _____)
h.	(called, lead)	(matter, tear)	(dagger, _____)
i.	(piper, ripe)	(mowed, dome)	(newts, _____)
j.	(clear, race)	(tread, date)	(dream, _____)
k.	(dare, read)	(rage, gear)	(post, _____)
l.	(and, sanded)	(eat, seated)	(had, _____)

Total: / 12

CHAPTER 5, SECTION C – LANGUAGE INFERENCE

The following extract is taken from the novel, Christy, by Catherine Marshall. In 1912, Christy, a nineteen-year-old girl, moves to Cutter Gap in the great Smoky Mountains in America to teach at a mission school. However, before she can reach the mission, she has to undergo a dangerous journey.

MR Pentland carried the mail to the Cove, and after much persuasion, allowed me to go along with him into the mountains to the school. He good-naturedly carried my valise along with his mail pack. Still, he wanted me to know that he meant business, so he was setting a brisk pace.

For the first half mile or so there was a wide, well-travelled lane which many feet had packed into a hard, white roadbed. One side was bordered by a row of giant spruces, black against the snow, their shadows long in the morning light.

Then we reached the edge of a large creek, and I saw that there was no real bridge across it, only a makeshift affair of two huge uneven logs with an occasional thin board nailed across. The whole contraption swayed precariously six feet or more high in the air above the water. I looked down at my boots and at my skirt, the mass of wet cloth clinging to my ankles. If only the logs were not so far above the water, and if only they had put the two logs closer together.

Mr Pentland said, "I'll go first to see it hits slippery-like. Then you'd better stomp your feet and get warm before you try it."

My eyes were on his feet. Halfway across he paused. Below him the water sprayed over the boulders in the middle of the stream where the water was not frozen. He called back, "It ain't bad. Wait until I get across though, so you won't get no sway."

Standing on the bank, I felt sick at my stomach. I never had liked heights. I heard Mr Pentland's voice above the roar of the water. "Stomp your feet now. Get 'em warm. Then come on - but first scrape your boots, then hoist your skirts."

Mechanically I did as he was directing me, then took a deep breath and put one foot on the log. It swayed a little and my boot sent a piece of bark flying into the water. I took a few steps, shut my eyes, then opened them again. Another step. Perhaps if I kept on looking at Mr Pentland waiting for me on the

other bank -- step - or kept my eyes on my valise - step - and did not once look below me - step - the sound of water became a roar in my ears. That meant I must be about halfway now.

I heard Mr Pentland's voice. "You're doin' fine. Keep a-comin'. Not far now."

Again the logs swayed. Each time I came to one of the cross-pieces, I was forced to look at my feet lest I trip over the edge of the board, and then in spite of myself I saw the water too. The logs were swaying, tilting... I dropped to my knees and began crawling. I hadn't thought it would be this bad! Dizzy...I felt dizzy. Mr Pentland was shouting at me. Dimly his voice penetrated, "Only a few more steps. Stand up now. I'll catch you."

Unsteadily I stood up again. The valise, keep my eyes on the valise ... Step - getting closer now, only a few more feet. Then at last I saw Mr Pentland's grinning face below me. "Guess you ain't crossed the likes of that before." He held out a gnarled hand and almost lifted me off the end of the log.

Questions

1. In your own words, explain why Mr Pentland set a "brisk pace". [1 mark]

Answer:_____

2. Describe the bridge across the creek? [2 marks]

Answer:_____

_____

3. Underline the correct answer. "Makeshift" means: [1 mark]

    a. moveable

    b. permanent

    c. temporary

    d. uneven

4. Underline the correct answer. "Swayed precariously" means: [1 mark]

    a. shook heavily

    b. swing gently

    c. swung dangerously

    d. rocked pleasantly

5. "If only…" What two things about the bridge does she wish were different about the bridge? [2 marks]

Answer:_____

_____

6. Underline the correct answer. "Wait until I get acrost though, so you won't get no sway." Mr Pentland means that Christy must wait until he crosses: [1 mark]

    a. so that the bridge won't break

    b. so that Christy cannot escape

    c. so that the bridge will swing from side to side

    d. so that the bridge will not swing from side to side

7. Why does Christy feel sick in the stomach? [1 mark]

Answer:_____

8. Why does Mr Pentland advise her to scrape her boots and hoist her skirts? [1 mark]

Answer:_____

9. What does Christy do in order to have the courage to walk halfway across? [1 mark]

Answer:_____

10. What happens that causes Christy to become dizzy? [1 mark]

Answer:_____

11. What does she do as soon as she becomes dizzy? [1 mark]

Answer:_____

12. Complete the following sentence by inserting two appropriate adjectives to describe Mr Pentland's attitude towards Christy throughout the crossing. [2 marks]

Mr Pentland was _____ and _____ towards Christy.

13. Write the meaning of the following words as they are used in the passage. [5 marks]

    a. valise _____

    b. brisk _____

c. creek _____

d. lest _____

e. gnarled _____

Total: / 20

My Chapter 5 Score: / 59 = _____ %

You're really progressing now. By learning about the order of operations you'll be better able to complete Maths problems as you move between primary and secondary education. You're developing a much better understanding of written text now too – and hopefully enjoying what you're reading more, as you better understand context, motivation, language choices and more.

CHAPTER 6

CHAPTER 6, SECTION A – MATHEMATICAL REASONING

Multiplying and Dividing with Decimals

Multiplying with decimals is easy if you follow this method and look for the number of digits after the decimal point.

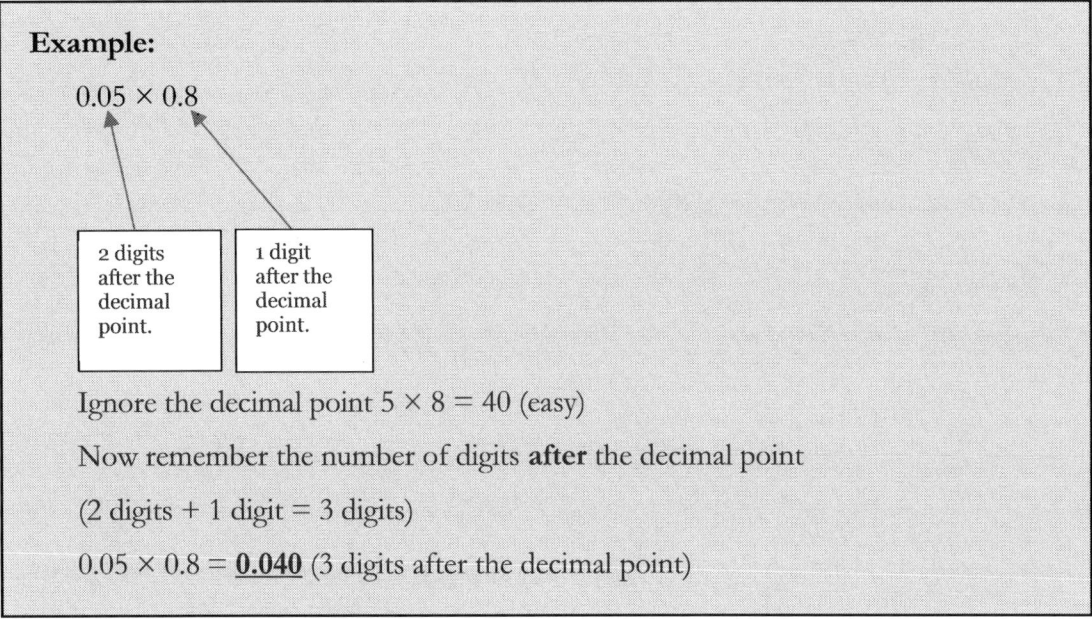

Example:

0.05×0.8

- 2 digits after the decimal point.
- 1 digit after the decimal point.

Ignore the decimal point $5 \times 8 = 40$ (easy)

Now remember the number of digits **after** the decimal point

(2 digits + 1 digit = 3 digits)

$0.05 \times 0.8 = \underline{\mathbf{0.040}}$ (3 digits after the decimal point)

Dividing by decimals is made easier if you remember your **equivalent fractions**.

Remember $\frac{4}{5}$ is the same as $4 \div 5$

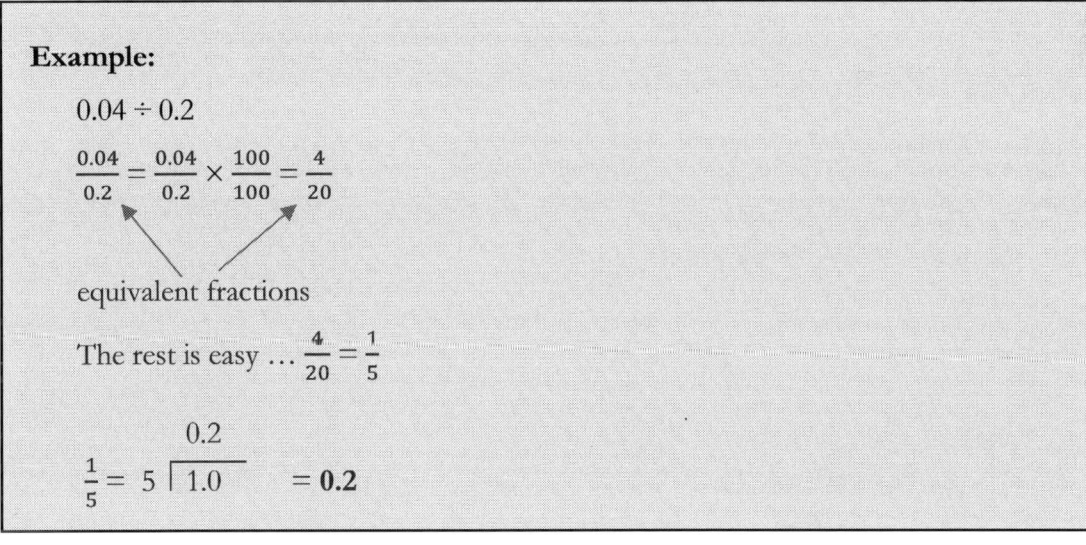

Example:

$0.04 \div 0.2$

$$\frac{0.04}{0.2} = \frac{0.04}{0.2} \times \frac{100}{100} = \frac{4}{20}$$

equivalent fractions

The rest is easy ... $\frac{4}{20} = \frac{1}{5}$

$\frac{1}{5} = 5 \overline{)1.0}^{\,0.2} = \mathbf{0.2}$

Questions

1. $0.5 \times 0.4 =$

Answer: _____

2. $0.84 \times 0.3 =$

Answer: _____

3. $6 \times 0.005 =$

Answer: _____

4. $200 \times 0.0065 =$

Answer: _____

5. $1.00005 \times 0.004 =$

Answer: _____

6. $0.06 \div 0.3 =$

Answer: _____

7. $0.48 \div 0.04 =$

Answer: _____

8. $8.4 \div 0.07 =$

Answer: _____

9. $87.5 \div 2.5 =$

Answer: _____

10. $0.00132 \div 0.11 =$

Answer: _____

11. A library is thinking about buying new books that cost £5.99 each. How much will it cost to buy 45 books?

Answer: _____

12. A rectangle measures 35.5cm by 15.03cm. What is the area of the rectangle?

Answer: _____

13. How many 0.05m lengths of wood can be cut from a plank of length 1.35m?

Answer: _____

14. Work out value of:

$$\frac{2.005 \times 4.8}{0.04}$$

Answer: _____

15. If a computer game costs £24.99, how many can I buy for £124.00?

Answer: _____

Total: / 15

CHAPTER 6, SECTION B – VERBAL REASONING

By finding the words in these exercises you are using your **decoding** skills and learning how to pay close attention to letters. By looking for a pattern in a set of numbers, you are looking for **logical sequences** to continue the series.

Questions

1. In each sentence below, one word, which is in capitals has no meaning because it has had **three consecutive letters** taken out. This **three**-letter word will make a correctly spelt word without changing the order and make the word in capitals make more sense. Write the **three-letter** word in the space provided.

Example.	John bought a new **COMER**.	(<u>put</u>)
a.	Jeremy was eating some **SWICHES**.	( )
b.	We grow **TOOES** in our greenhouse.	( )
c.	I received three **TERS** this morning.	( )
d.	**TENS** are just young cats.	( )
e.	The **PR** of the book was £1.	( )
f.	It is very **PEFUL** in the countryside.	( )
g.	The train will **DEP** in ten minutes.	( )
h.	My friend David is **BRIANT** at football.	( )

i.	Dad was **MING** the broken window.	( )
j.	The **FER** owned lots of animals.	( )
k.	The prisoner **ESED** from the jail.	( )
l.	In a few **MIES** the test will start.	( )

Total: / 12

2. You are given a list of numbers that form a series with a logical sequence. Write down the number that continues the series in the most sensible way in the space provided.

Example.	5, 10, 15, 20, 25, (<u>30</u>)
a.	8, 8, 9, 11, 14, 18, (_____)
b.	23, 27, 31, 35, 39, (_____)
c.	97, 90, 84, 79, 75, 72, (_____)
d.	3, 9, 10, 30, 31, 93, (_____)
e.	1, 2, 4, 8, 16, 32, (_____)
f.	5, 9, 17, 29, 45, 65, (_____)
g.	32, 30, 29, 29, 30, 32, (_____)
h.	87, 82, 77, 72, 67, 62, (_____)
i.	30, 37, 31, 36, 32, 35, (_____)
j.	8, (_____), 15, 20, 26, 33, 41
k.	(_____), 8, 7, 10, 9, 12, 11
l.	85, 84, 80, (_____), 63, 50, 34

Total: / 12

CHAPTER 6, SECTION C – LANGUAGE INFERENCE

The following diary extract is taken from the novel, <u>Dracula</u>, by Bram Stoker. Use your language inference skills to find meaning in the text.

5 MAY. I must have been asleep, for certainly if I had been fully awake I must have noticed the approach of such a remarkable place. In the gloom the courtyard looked of considerable size, and as several dark ways led from it under great round arches, it perhaps seemed bigger than it really is. I have not yet been able to see it by daylight.

When the carriage stopped, the driver jumped down and held out his hand to assist me to alight. As I stood, the driver jumped again into his seat and shook the reins. The horses started forward, and carriage and all disappeared down one of the dark openings.

I stood in silence where I was, for I did not know what to do. Of bell or knocker there was no sign. The time I waited seemed endless, and I felt doubts and fears crowding upon me. What sort of place had I come to, and among what kind of people? What sort of grim adventure was it on which I had embarked?

I began to rub my eyes and pinch myself to see if I were awake. It all seemed like a horrible nightmare to me, and I expected that I should suddenly awake, and find myself at home.

Suddenly, I heard a heavy step approaching behind the great door, and saw through the chinks the gleam of a coming light. Then there was the sound of rattling chains and the clanking of massive bolts drawn back. A key was turned with the loud grating noise of long disuse, and the great door swung back.

Within, stood a tall old man, clean shaven save for a long white moustache, and clad in black from head to foot, without a single speck of colour about him anywhere. He held in his hand an antique silver lamp. The old man motioned me in with his right hand with a courtly gesture, saying in excellent English, but with a strange accent:

"Welcome to my house! Enter freely and of your own free will!" The instant that I had stepped over the threshold, he moved impulsively forward, and holding out his hand grasped mine with a strength which made me wince, an effect which was not lessened by the fact that it seemed cold as ice, more like the hand of a dead than a living man.

I asked interrogatively, "Count Dracula?"

He bowed in a courtly way as he replied, "I am Dracula, and I bid you welcome to my house.

Questions

1. Underline the correct answer. What does the courtyard was of "considerable size" mean? [1 mark]

    a. worthy of consideration.

    b. worth a great deal of money.

    c. very large in size.

    d. designed in a good manner.

2. What doubts and fears does the narrator have? [3 marks]

Answer:_____

_____

_____

3. Why does he pinch himself? [2 marks]

Answer:_____

_____

4. What four sounds does the narrator hear before the door opens? [4 marks]

Answer:_____

_____

_____

_____

5. Describe in your own words the man who opens the door. [4 marks]

Answer:_____

_____

_____

_____

_____

6. Underline the correct answer. The phrase "motioned me in with a courtly gesture" means? [1 mark]

    a.   in a polite manner.

    b.   in a manner like a judge.

    c.   with a strict look in his face.

    d.   without moving much,

7. What two things are unusual about his handshake? [2 marks]

Answer:_____

8. Write the meaning of the following words as they are used in the passage. [3 marks]

    a.   remarkable_____

    b.   chinks _____

    c.   grim _____

Total: / 20

My Chapter 6 Score: / 59 = _____ %

By the end of chapter six, you will be mastering Verbal and Mathematical Reasoning and Inference – harnessing the skills and knowledge you will need for any secondary entrance examination. Multiplying with decimals is a particularly tricky concept, so keep this, using the method outlined in this chapter to help you better understand how you're solving problems.

CHAPTER 7

CHAPTER 7, SECTION A – MATHEMATICAL REASONING

Percentages

'Per cent' means 'out of 100', so 20% means 20 out of 100. **Percentage**s are useful because people can compare things that are not out of the same number. For example, exam marks are often percentages, so people can compare them even if there are more questions on one exam paper than the other.

Percentages can be expressed as fractions or decimals.

Example: $45\% = \frac{45}{100} = \frac{9}{20} = \mathbf{0.45}$

Remember the following:

Decimal	Fraction	Percentage
1.0	$\frac{1}{1}$	100%
0.75	$\frac{3}{4}$	75%
0.50	$\frac{1}{2}$	50%
0.333	$\frac{1}{3}$	33.3%
0.25	$\frac{1}{4}$	25%
0.20	$\frac{1}{5}$	20%
0.125	$\frac{1}{8}$	12.5%
0.11	$\frac{1}{10}$	10%

Examples:

What is 5% of 20?

$\frac{5}{100} \times 20 = \underline{1}$

What is 20% of 500?

$\frac{20}{100} \times 500 = \underline{100}$ or $1\% = \frac{1}{100} \times 500 = 5$, then $20\% = 20 \times 5 = \underline{100}$

Questions

1. Write each percentage as a fraction in its lowest terms. [5 marks]

    a. 15%

Answer: _____

    b. 60%

Answer: _____

    c. 35%

Answer: _____

    d. 12%

Answer: _____

    e. 150%

Answer: _____

2. Write each decimal as a percentage. [5 marks]

    a. 0.1

Answer: _____

    b. 0.16

Answer: _____

    c. 0.845

Answer: _____

d. 1.0

Answer: _____

e. 1.72

Answer: _____

3. There are 250 pupils in a sixth form. 40% were female. How many were male? [1 mark]

Answer: _____

4. The Maths department had to update its textbooks as 2% of its books were too damaged. If it had 1,650 books, how many were damaged? [1 mark]

Answer: _____

5. Stuart set up a revision timetable for his exams. He is going to spend 10% of his time on English, 35% on Maths, 12% on French and the rest on Science. What percentage of his time is he going to spend on Science? [1 mark]

Answer: _____

6. James gave 12 ½ % of his 'penny' sweets to his sister. If he had 48 sweets in total, how many did he give to his sister? [1 mark]

Answer: _____

7. Alex has a bar of chocolate. He eats 50% on Monday, 20% of what was left on Tuesday and 10% of what was left on Wednesday. What percentage of his bar of chocolate did Alex have left for Thursday? [1 mark]

Answer: _____

Total: / 15

CHAPTER 7, SECTION B – VERBAL REASONING

Use your **decoding** skills to solve the following equations.

Questions

1. Letters stand for numbers in the questions below. Write the answer as a **letter** in the space provided.

Example.	A = 2, B = 3, C = 4, D = 5, E = 1 So, A + B – E =	(C)
a.	A = 2, B = 4, C = 6, D = 10, E = 12 So, A + B + C =	( )
b.	A = 3, B = 6, C = 9, D = 10, E = 12 So, B + C – E =	( )
c.	A = 4, B = 5, C = 6, D = 10, E = 25 So, A + B + C – D =	( )
d.	A = 6, B = 7, C = 8, D = 10, E = 11 So, B + D – E =	( )
e.	A = 22, B = 4, C = 5, D = 15, E = 13 So, A – B – C =	( )
f.	A = 10, B = 6, C = 5, D = 7, E = 12 So, E + C – D =	( )
g.	A = 16, B = 14, C = 6, D = 8, E = 12 So, B + C + D – E =	( )
h.	A = 9, B = 6, C = 16, D = 18, E = 19 So, A + C – B =	( )
i.	A = 32, B = 34, C = 6, D = 10, E – 12 So, A + E – D =	( )

j.	A = 2, B = 4, C = 6, D = 10, E = 12 So, A + B + C – D =	( )
k.	A = 30, B = 4, C = 20, D = 10, E = 50 So, B × C – E =	( )
l.	A = 10, B = 9, C = 11, D = 13, E = 12 So, A – B + C =	( )

2. Underline the **two** words, **one from each set**, that together make **one** correctly spelt word, without changing the order of the letters. **The word from the first set always comes first.**

Example.	(<u>motor</u> gas electric)	(engine bus <u>cycle</u>)
a.	(small thin smack)	(king boy man)
b.	(no not cloth)	(wear some thing)
c.	(bean carrot pea)	(leaf nut top)
d.	(steal beg ask)	(on out in)
e.	(not never new)	(ice snow hail)
f.	(point direct show)	(or are met)
g.	(day weak week)	(tip top end)
h.	(chair desk bed)	(table room seat)
i.	(with able trip)	(on out up)
j.	(over into under)	(sit crouch stand)
k.	(import export sport)	(bug ant fly)
l.	(no go so)	(leg are wing)

Total: / 24

CHAPTER 7, SECTION C – LANGUAGE INFERENCE

The following extract is taken from the novel, Treasure Island, by Robert Louis Stevenson. The narrator is being chased by a gang of pirates when the events of the passage take place. Use your language skills to help you understand what's going on in the text.

FROM the side of the hill, which was steep and stony, a spout of gravel was dislodged, and fell rattling and bounding through the trees. My eyes turned instinctively in the direction, and I saw a figure leap with great rapidity behind the trunk of a pine. What it was, whether bear or man or monkey, I could not tell.

It seemed dark and shaggy; more I knew not. But the terror of this new apparition brought me to a stand.

I was now, it seemed, cut off upon both sides; behind me the murderers, before me this lurking nondescript. And immediately I began to prefer the dangers that I knew to those I knew not. The pirates themselves appeared less terrible in contrast with this creature of the woods, and I turned on my heel, and looking sharply behind me over my shoulder, began to retract my steps in the direction of the boats.

Instantly the figure reappeared, and, making a wide circuit began to head me off. I was tired and I could see it was in vain for me to contend in speed with such an adversary. From trunk to trunk the creature flitted like a deer, running manlike on two legs but unlike any man that I had ever seen, stooping almost double as it ran. Yet a man it was, I could no longer be in doubt about that.

I began to recall what I had heard of cannibals. I was within an ace of calling for help. But the mere fact that he was man, however wild, somewhat reassured me. I stood still therefore and cast about for some method of escape; and as I was so thinking, the recollection of my pistol flashed into my mind. As soon as I remembered I was not defenceless, courage glowed again in my heart; and I set my face resolutely for this man of the island and walked briskly towards him.

He was concealed by this time, behind another tree trunk, but he must have been watching me closely, for as soon as I began to move in his direction he reappeared and took a step to meet me. Then he hesitated, drew back, came forward again, and at last, to my wonder and confusion, threw himself on his knees and held out his clasped hands in supplication.

At that I once more stopped.

"Who are you?" I asked.

"Ben Gunn," he answered, and his voice sounded hoarse and awkward, like a rusty lock. "I'm poor Ben Gunn, I am; and I haven't spoken with any person these three years."

His skin, wherever it was exposed, was burnt by the sun; even his lips were black; and his fair eyes looked quite startling in so dark a face. He was clothed with tatters of old ship's canvas and old sea cloth; and this extraordinary patchwork was all held together by a system of fastenings, brass buttons, bits of stick, and loops of animal skin. About his waist he wore an old brass-buckled leather belt.

"Three years!" I cried.

"Were you shipwrecked?"

"Nay, mate," said he, "- marooned."

I had heard the word, and I knew it stood for a horrible kind of punishment common enough among the buccaneers, in which the offender is put ashore with a little ammunition, and left behind on some desolate and distant island.

Questions

1. What causes the "spout of gravel" to be dislodged? [1 mark]

Answer:_____

2. Why do you think the figure leapt behind the trunk of a pine? [1 mark]

Answer:_____

3. The narrator's terror brings him "to a stand". What does this mean? [1 mark]

Answer:_____

4. Why does the narrator decide to retreat to the boats? [1 mark]

Answer:_____

5. The creature "flitted like a deer". What does this tell us about the way the stranger moved? [1 mark]

Answer:_____

6. What thought gives the narrator courage? [1 mark]

Answer:_____

7. How does the stranger react when the narrator walks towards him? [2 marks]

Answer:_____

_____

8. Underline the correct answer. "Held out his clasped hands in supplication" means? [1 mark]

   a. showing his fists

   b. about to faint with fear

   c. showing he isn't carrying a weapon

   d. begging for help

9. Underline the correct answer. "His voice sounded hoarse and awkward, like a rusty lock." This figure of speech is? [1 mark]

   a. a simile

   b. personification

   c. onomatopoeia

   d. alliteration

10. Why is his voice hoarse and awkward? [1 mark]

Answer:_____

11. Describe Ben Gunn's clothing. [3 marks]

Answer:_____

_____

_____

12. In your own words, describe what "marooned" means? [3 marks]

Answer:_____

_____

_____

13. Write the meaning of the following words as they are used in the passage. [5 marks]

   a. rapidity _____

   b. apparition _____

c. concealed _____

d. hoarse _____

e. buccaneers _____

Total: / 22

My Chapter 7 Score: / 61 = _____ %

As well as further improving your ability to understand and decode language, in chapter seven you've learnt about percentages - a powerful way to compare samples with different numbers of observations. Many children find working with percentages tricky, so keep these exercises!

CHAPTER 8

CHAPTER 8, SECTION A – MATHEMATICAL REASONING

Perimeter, Area and Volume

Perimeter means the distance all the way around a shape. Remember the distance around a circle is called the **circumference**.

Area of a shape is found by multiplying the length and breadth.

Total surface area means the area of each side of a 3-D shape added together.

Volume of a shape is found by multiplying the length, breadth and height. (This can also be found by multiplying the cross-sectional surface area by the depth or height).

Remember your units of measurement:

- Perimeter (cm)
- Area (cm²)
- Volume (cm³)

Examples:

1. Find the perimeter and area of the shape below.

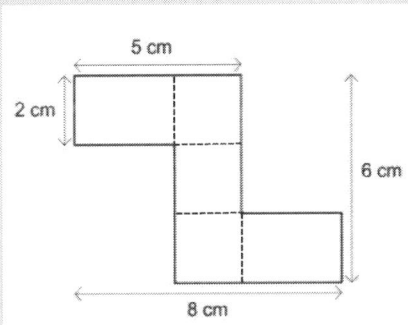

Perimeter = 5 + 4 + 3 + 2 + 5 + 4 + 3 + 2 = **28cm**

Area = L × W = (5 × 2) + (2 × 2) + (6 × 2) = **26cm²**

2. Find the volume of the shape below.

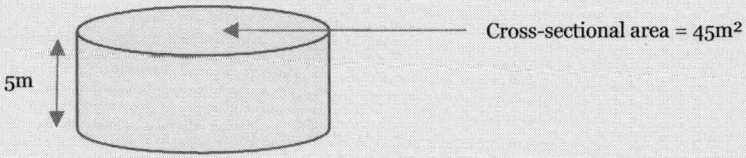

Volume = Cross-sectional area × depth = 45 × 5 = **225cm³**

Questions

1&2. Fill in the blanks in the table below. [10 marks]

1.	Length	Breadth	Perimeter of rectangle	Area of rectangle
a.	15cm	8cm	___cm	___cm²
b.	___m	12m	44m	___m²
c.	11mm	___mm	___mm	55mm²
d.	85cm	50mm	___cm	___cm²
e.	___cm	3m	___cm	1500cm²

2.	Length	Breadth	Height	Volume of cuboid
a.	15cm	10cm	4cm	___cm³
b.	___cm	50cm	1cm	400cm³
c.	5m	___m	12m	720m³
d.	45m	300cm	200mm	___m³
e.	95cm	25.5cm	12cm	___cm³

3. If I draw a rectangle with sides 18cm and 36cm. How many squares of side 4cm would fit exactly in it? [1 mark]

Answer: _____

4. My dad is paving the patio using slabs that measure 100cm by 50cm. How many slabs does he need to cover an area 6.6m by 10m? [1 mark]

Answer: _____

5. A metal cylinder has a cross-sectional area of 82cm². What is the volume of the cylinder if it is 22.5cm high? [1 mark]

Answer: _____

6. A prism has a triangular cross-section that has a base of 4m and perpendicular height of 1.25m. If the prism is 20m deep, what is its volume? [1 mark]

Answer: _____

7. An empty container measures 15m × 9m × 7m. How many cubes of side 3m will fit exactly into the box? [1 mark]

Answer: _____

Total: / 15

CHAPTER 8, SECTION B – VERBAL REASONING

Understanding the concept of opposites and similarities is important as it helps you learn how to compare two different things and to develop a more concrete understanding of a specific concept (e.g. hard vs soft). Learning opposites also improves your ability to describe things.

Questions

1. Find and underline **two** words, **one from each group**, that are **opposite** in meaning.

Example.	(<u>up</u> run walk)	(smile laugh <u>down</u>)
a.	(top middle cork)	(chair seat bottom)
b.	(giant talk tall)	(bean trim short)
c.	(line live cross)	(nothing die never)
d.	(through under inside)	(outside between back)
e.	(awake alive answer)	(tired naughty snoozing)
f.	(few front side)	(forward many inside)
g.	(small first second)	(runner minute last)
h.	(unhappy naughty silly)	(annoyed cheerful pleased)
i.	(knew new start)	(old sold begin)
j.	(broad bottom top)	(raise narrow lower)
k.	(lower raise move)	(bottom higher lean)
l.	(small hard round)	(easy tiny smooth)

Total: / 12

2. The three words in the second group should go together in the same way as the three in the first group. Find the missing word from the second group and write it in the space provided.

Example.	lint [liner] term
	drop [drove] even
a.	file [list] sat
	beds [_____] nut
b.	bond [moan] same
	yell [_____] cart
c.	stay [best] beam
	apes [_____] tree
d.	slip [pale] lace
	over [_____] name
e.	bike [sack] cash
	send [_____] walk
f.	tale [lame] milk
	dune [_____] lark
g.	date [lace] calm
	much [_____] tame
h.	stem [last] call
	area [_____] near
i.	lead [sold] lost
	mole [_____] bath

j.	bald [made] team free [_____] owed
k.	plan [lean] hole road [_____] ogre

Total: / 11

CHAPTER 8, SECTION C – LANGUAGE INFERENCE

The following newspaper article reports on the Mozambique floods which occurred in February and March 2000. Use your language inference skills to understand the meaning of the extract.

INITIALLY, the only sign of life in southern Mozambique is an arm thrust from among the leaves of trees that scatter the flooded landscape. The anonymous limb waves a cooking pot, not with any great vigour, for fear of upsetting the balance. But this is all it takes for a rescue worker in the air to see.

The helicopter moves in to save another person from the worst floods in living memory. The gale pumped out by its rotors opens the tree like a flower, pushing the leaves and branches aside to reveal eight people perched high above the water. It is a precarious business for everyone involved. The exhausted Mozambicans must hold on tighter than ever to prevent the helicopter's wind tossing them into the water. The pilot has to get close enough to winch down one of the crew, without letting the tail collide with the tree.

The fear of the moment is written over the elderly face of Celeste Libombo. She has little choice but to put her faith in the man lowered to grab her. Eventually she is torn from the vegetation that had been her home for five days and hauled aboard the helicopter. She sits on the floor, stunned.

But people are not the only ones living in trees. Millions of insects seek refuge in the foliage. For them too it is a matter of life and death. Libombo says her clothes and head were covered in bugs for days.

"Sometimes I couldn't open my eyes because the insects crawled into them. We poured water over ourselves to get them off, but they always came back," she said. "There was no food, and drinking the water made me sick."

A greater danger lurks in the greenery - snakes. Green mambas are particularly feared as they wriggle through the water in search of safety among the trees or slivers of high ground packed with people. An accurate aim with a sling shot can stun a snake long enough to allow someone to beat it to death. Everyone knows that a single bite, with no means of treating it, is a death sentence.

Clinging to a tree for a long period of time is no small feat and many have been injured due to the ordeal. The helicopters are few and those in need of rescue great. Loss of life is inevitable.

Not all the tree dwellers are grateful to see the helicopters. Some people furiously wave them away. Perhaps they fear being thrown out of their tree. It is more likely that they do not want to abandon what little they have left. From the branches, many people can see their homes. When the waters subside they will go home, rescue what they can and start replanting crops. But the weather report tells us that more rain is expected and that cyclone Gloria is hovering menacingly around the Mozambique channel. The nightmare may yet grow in intensity!

Questions

1. Why did the "anonymous limb" not wave the cooking pot vigorously? [1 mark]

Answer:_____

2. "The gale pumped out by its rotors opens the tree like a flower." Underline what figure of speech this is: [1 mark]

    a. metaphor

    b. simile

    c. onomatopoeia

    d. alliteration

3. Underline the correct answer: "it is a precarious business for everyone involved" means: [1 mark]

    a. everyone involved hated doing it

    b. it was a dangerous situation for everyone

    c. everyone was balancing in the tree

    d. the helicopter made everyone feel afraid

4. Why were there so many bugs? [1 mark]

Answer:_____

5. Name three hardships that Celeste Libombo had to endure during her days in the tree. [3 marks]

Answer:_____

6. Why are green mambas "particularly feared"? [1 mark]

Answer:_____

7. Underline the correct answer. What is a "slingshot"? [1 mark]

    a. a gunshot

    b. a cloth bandage

    c. a catapult

d. a spear

8. "The nightmare may yet grow in intensity!" What is meant by this? [1 mark]

Answer:_____

9. Give a synonym for the following words as they are used in the passage. [5 marks]

a. anonymous _____

b. reveal _____

c. foliage _____

d. grateful _____

e. menacing _____

10. The following passage is taken from another news article about the hurricane. Fill in the appropriate words from the spelling bank below:

| devastated | eventually | countries | independence | effects |
| experienced | imagination | recovering | tragedy | cyclone |

The _____ is that Mozambique, one of the world's poorest _____, was _____ from the _____ of almost 16 years of civil war following _____ from Portugal in 1975 and is now being _____ by violent winds and rains. Not long ago, Maputo school children were given a project on using their _____ to describe a flood or a _____. When the children _____ return to their schools; those that have not been washed away or buried in the mud, will have sadly _____ the real thing. [10 marks]

Understanding and Applying: Mathematical Reasoning, Verbal Reasoning and Language Inference

Total: / 25

My Chapter 8 Score: / 53 = _____ %

We're getting to the end of the exercises now, and you're making fantastic progress. By completing these tasks you're mastering the reasoning skills you'll need for a smooth transition between primary and secondary education. As well as learning new Mathematical skills, you've improved your ability to understand the written word, gaining knowledge of meaning, language and context in writing.

CHAPTER 9

CHAPTER 9, SECTION A – MATHEMATICAL REASONING

Ratios

A ratio is the quantitative relation between two amounts showing the number of times one value contains or is contained within the other. More simply, it's a way of sharing a quantity.

Example:

1. Share 300 sweets in the ratio 7 : 3.
   Work out how many equal parts are needed: $7 + 3 = 10$
   Divide the quantity to share by the number of parts: $300 \div 10 = 30$

   So, 7 parts = $7 \times 30 = 210$
   3 parts = $3 \times 30 = 90$
   Answer: The sweets should be shared in the ratio **210 : 90**

   Remember when working with a ratio and different units (e.g. grams and kilograms), always change them to a common unit **first** before simplifying.

Example:

1. Express the ratio of 300g to 2.1kg in its simplest form
   Convert 2.1 kg to grams first
   300 : 2100
   3 : 21 (divide both sides by 100)
   1 : 7 (divide both sides by 3)
   Answer: In its simplest form the ratio of the weights is **1 : 7**

Questions

1. Share £6.00 in the ratio 3 : 2 [1 mark]

Answer: _____

2. Share 243g in the ratio 2 : 1 [1 mark]

Answer: _____

3. Share 605 in the ratio 2 : 3 [1 mark]

Answer: _____

4. Share £12.60 in the ratio 4 : 2 [1 mark]

Answer: _____

5. Share 195 in the ratio 7 : 4 : 2 [1 mark]

Answer: _____

6. Express 85g to 1kg in its simplest form. [1 mark]

Answer: _____

7. Express £3.50 to 50p in its simplest form. [1 mark]

Answer: _____

8. Express 0.1m to 500cm in its simplest form. [1 mark]

Answer: _____

9. Express 5 days to 1 year (assume it is not a leap year) in its simplest form. [1 mark]

Answer: _____

10. Express 4 hours to 1 day in its simplest form. [1 mark]

Answer: _____

11. The recipe for a cake is 125g sugar, 175g flour and 100g butter. A cake this size would feed 5 people. If I wanted to bake a cake for 20 people, how would my recipe change? [1 mark]

Answer: _____

12. Harry shared his marbles with Callum in the ratio 8 : 5. If Harry had 48 marbles after sharing them out, how many marbles were there in total? [1 mark]

Answer: _____

13. A map has a scale of 2cm to 5km. Express this scale as a ratio in its simplest form. [1 mark]

Answer: _____

14. Using the same map as in (Q. 13), how long in real life would a road be that measures 13 cm on the map? (Give your answer in km) [1 mark]

Answer: _____

15. My mum tells me that I have to split the rest of my day in the ratio 3 : 4 : 1 between playing, studying and reading. If I have 2 hours and 40 minutes left before I have to go to bed, how long do I have to spend studying? [1 mark]

Answer: _____ hr _____ mins

Total: / 15

CHAPTER 9, SECTION B – VERBAL REASONING

By completing these calculations, you will continue to improve your ability to look for **patterns** in number **sequences**. By finding similar meaning, you will improve your understanding of language and ability to use it creatively.

Questions

1. Find the number that will complete the sum correctly. Write out the answer in the space provided.

Example.	$4 \times 3 + 3 = 6 + 4 + [\;\underline{5}\;]$
a.	$19 - 6 + 2 = 28 + [\;\_\_\_\;] - 15$
b.	$24 - 10 + 6 = 8 + 7 + [\;\_\_\_\;]$
c.	$12 + 9 + 8 = 40 - [\;\_\_\_\;] + 9$
d.	$5 \times 3 + 10 = 11 + 12 + [\;\_\_\_\;]$
e.	$40 \div 10 - 1 = [\;\_\_\_\;] - 13 - 4$
f.	$7 \times 4 + 2 = 5 \times [\;\_\_\_\;] - 5$
g.	$9 \times 9 + 9 = 10 \times 10 - [\;\_\_\_\;]$
h.	$80 - 42 + 5 = 8 \times [\;\_\_\_\;] + 3$
i.	$48 - 18 - 7 = [\;\_\_\_\;] \times 3 + 2$
j.	$4 \times 5 \times 5 = 33 + [\;\_\_\_\;] + 32$
k.	$21 + 7 + 3 = 4 \times 5 + [\;\_\_\_\;]$
l.	$38 - 12 - 8 = 50 - 25 - [\;\_\_\_\;]$

Total: / 12

2. Find one word from the list in each question below that will go equally well with the **two pairs of words**.

Example.	*OFFICE CHAIN BEACH FARM STABLE* *(STEADY FIRM) (BARN SHED)*	(<u>STABLE</u>)
a.	*BUSH CEMENT GUM STICK TREE* *(TWIG BRANCH) (GLUE PASTE)*	(_____)
b.	*BUTTON GRIP GRAB HANDLE LOCK* *(HOLD TOUCH) (LEVER KNOB)*	(_____)
c.	*TELL INSTRUCT TROLLEY COACH RAIL* *(TEACH TRAIN) (BUS TRAM)*	(_____)
d.	*PITCH ARENA COLLUDE FIELD PLOT* *(AREA PATCH) (PLAN CONSPIRACY)*	(_____)
e.	*DISCO BALL EARTH BAT DROP* *(SPHERE GLOBE) (DANCE PARTY)*	(_____)
f.	*HOLD KEEP BOOK VOLUME TALE* *(RESERVE ORDER) (NOVEL STORY)*	(_____)
g.	*TIP STOPPED UNDER OVER POINT* *(ABOVE ON TOP) (FINISHED ENDED)*	(_____)

h.	ORANGE SQUASH SQUISH LEMON HIT (JUICE DRINK) (FLATTEN SPLATTER)	(_____)
i.	BOOK SAND BRUSH FILE WALLET (SCRAPE RUB) (FOLDER BINDER)	(_____)
j.	JAR LET CAN BOX TUB (TIN CONTAINER) (PERMITTED ALLOWED)	(_____)
k.	BRIGHT SMART GENIUS SUNNY LIGHT (SPARKLING SHINY) (INTELLIGENT CLEVER)	(_____)
l.	TOP END CEASE COMPLETE CHANGE (STOP FINISH) (TIP POINT)	(_____)

Total: /12

CHAPTER 9, SECTION C - LANGUAGE INFERENCE

The following extract is a description of an octopus hunt in the Gilbert Islands in the Pacific Ocean taken from the book A Pattern of Islands by Arthur Grimble. Use your inference skills to understand the text.

THE Gilbertese happen to value certain parts of the octopus as food. They hunt for it in pairs. One man acts as bait, his partner as the killer. First, they swim eyes-under at low tide just off the reef, and search the crannies of the submarine cliff for sight of any tentacle that may flicker out for a catch. When they have located their quarry, they land on the reef for the next stage. The human bait starts the real game. He dives and tempts the lurking brute by swimming a few strokes in front of its cranny, at first a little beyond striking range. Then he turns and swims straight for the cranny, to give himself into the embrace of those waiting arms.

The partner on the reef above stares down through the water, waiting for his moment. His killing efficiency depends on his avoiding every one of those strangling arms. He dives, lays hold of his pinioned friend at arm's length; the octopus is torn from the anchorage, and clamps itself the more fiercely to its prey. In the same second, the human bait gives a kick, which brings him, with his quarry, to the surface. He turns on his back, still holding his breath for better buoyancy, and this exposes the body of the beast for the kill. The killer closes in, grasps the evil head from behind, and wrenches it away from its meal and kills it. That is the end of it. It dies on the instant; the suckers release their hold; the arms fall away; the two fishers paddle with whoops of delighted laughter to the reef, where they string the catch to a pole before going to rout out the next one.

Any two boys of seventeen, any day of the week, will go out and get you half a dozen octopus like that for the mere fun of it. Here lies the whole point of this story. The hunt is, in the most literal sense, nothing but child's play to the Gilbertese.

As I was standing one day at the end of the jetty in Tarawa lagoon, I saw two boys from the nearby village shouldering a string of octopus slung on a pole between them...Then they began whispering together. I knew in a curdling flash what they were saying to each other... I was already known as a young Man of Matang who liked swimming, and fishing and laughing with the villagers; I had just shown an interest in this particular form of hunting; naturally, I should enjoy the fun of it as much as they did. Without even waiting for my answer, they gleefully ducked off the edge of the reef to look for another octopus - a fine, fat one – *mine*.

I hope I did not look as yellow as I felt when I stood to take the plunge; I have never been so sick with nerves before or since.

Questions

1. Why do the Gilbertese hunt octopus in pairs? [2 marks]

Answer:_____   _____

_____

2. "They swim eyes-under." What does this expression mean? [1 mark]

Answer:_____

3. In your own words, describe how the one partner acts as the "human bait". [2 marks]

Answer:_____

_____

4. Find TWO different words in the first paragraph that the author uses instead of the word "octopus". [2 marks]

_____ and _____

5. Give a reason why the partner with the octopus turns onto his back when he reaches the surface. [1 mark]

Answer:_____

6. What does "… the evil head" tell us about the author's feelings about the octopus? [1 mark]

Answer:_____

7. Underline the correct answer. "they string the catch to a pole before going **to rout out** the next one." The words in bold mean: [1 mark]

    a. to celebrate

    b. to uncover

    c. to riot

    d. to swim

8. Underline the correct answer. "The hunt is, in the most **literal** sense." Literal means: [1 mark]

    a. imaginary

    b. actual

    c. figurative

    d. free

9. Why is hunting octopus like child's play to the Gilbertese? [1 mark]

Answer:_____

10. Why do the Gilbertese think that the author would enjoy octopus hunting? [2 marks]

Answer:_____

_____

11. Why did the author feel "yellow" before he dived? [1 mark]

Answer:_____

12. What does the saying "to take the plunge" mean? [1 mark]

Answer:_____

13. Give a synonym for the following words as they are used in the passage. [3 marks]

    a. crannies _____

    b. gleefully _____

    c. flash _____ _____

Total: / 19

My Chapter 9 Score: / 58 = _____ %

In chapter nine we learnt about ratios. A tricky concept for some, ratios occur frequently in daily life and help to simplify many of our interactions by putting numbers into perspective. Ratios allow us to measure and express quantities by making them easier to understand – and you'll use them time and again both in the classroom and out. Your reasoning skills are improving all the time – well done!

CHAPTER 10

CHAPTER 10. SECTION A – MATHEMATICAL REASONING

Number Sequences

A **sequence** is a set of numbers or patterns linked by a rule. Each number in the sequence is called a **term**. The rule helps you to find the next number or pattern in the sequence

Types of Sequences

1. ODD AND EVEN – each term in the sequence is either odd or even.

2. ARITHMETIC – each term in the sequence is made by adding or subtracting a value to the previous term.

   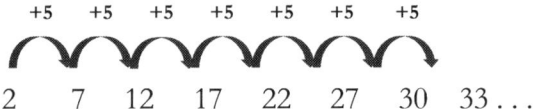

3. GEOMETRIC – each term in the sequence is made by multiplying or dividing a value to the previous term.

   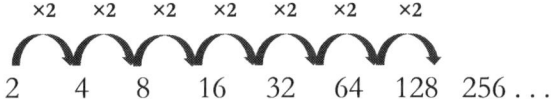

4. CHANGING NUMBER – where the value changes with each step.

   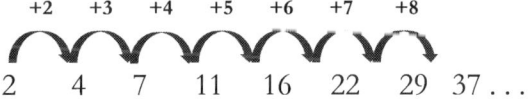

5. REPEATED PATTERN – where the pattern is repeated after a number of steps.

6. **FIBONACCI NUMBERS** – where the next term is found by adding the previous two terms.

    0   1   1   2   3   5   8   13   21   34

In a sequence where the difference between each term is the same, for example +2 or -2, then a general rule or expression can be found, where the position of the term in a sequence is **n** and each term is ***x***.

For example:

Position (n)	1	2	3	4	5
Term (*x*)	5	8	11	14	17

Each term in the sequence is made by adding the value **+3**.
Now **take away 3** from the first term which is 5 – 3 = 2

So the expression for this sequence is 3n + 2
Now if I want to know the 100th term in the sequence: 3(100) + 2 = 302.

Questions

1. Look at the sequences below and find the next 2 numbers in the sequence. [4 marks]

   a. 9, 12, 15, 18, 21 _____ , _____

   b. 3, 6, 12, 24 _____ , _____

   c. -4, -9, -14, -19 _____ , _____

   d. 8, 10, 18, 28, 46, _____ , _____

2. Look at the sequences below and explain the rule that links the numbers. [3 marks]

   a. 9, 27, 81, 243. The rule is: _____

   b. 375, 75, 15, 3, 0.6. The rule is: _____

   c. 1, 3, 4, 7, 11, 18. The rule is: _____

Understanding and Applying: Mathematical Reasoning, Verbal Reasoning and Language Inference

3. Find the *n*th term in each sequence. [3 marks]

{Remember this means finding a rule that allows you to work out the value of any term in the sequence. Example: In the expression 3n + 2, the value of the 5th term = 3 × 5 + 2 = 17.}

   a. 8, 12, 16, 20, 24

   b. 1, 9, 17, 25, 33

   c. 6, 2, -2, -6, -10

4. Find the value of the 100th term in each sequence. [3 marks]

   a. 2, 12, 22, 32, 42

   b. 13, 16, 19, 22, 25

   c. 4, 1, -2, -5, -8

Total: / 13

CHAPTER 10, SECTION B – VERBAL REASONING

When you rearrange letters to make new words, you are looking closely at those words and letters to improve your ability to manipulate them. The same is true when you look at **relationships** between letters.

Questions

1. **One** letter from the word on the left must be moved into the word on the right to make **two new words**. The letters must not be re-arranged. **Both new words must make sense**. Write the two new words in the spaces provided.

Example.	CLIMB	LOSE	LIMB	CLOSE	(C)
a.	PLANE	FAR			
b.	FLAME	SIP			
c.	PAINT	RED			
d.	CRAFT	ART			
e.	BLACK	TIE			
f.	CRASH	OWED			
g.	BLEND	OLD			
h.	STINK	BUS			
i.	TEASE	SPIN			
j.	IDEAL	PACE			
k.	DRAFT	MEN			
l.	TABLE	EAST			

Total: / 12

Understanding and Applying: Mathematical Reasoning, Verbal Reasoning and Language Inference

2. Find the letters that will complete the sentence in the best way.

A B C D E F G H I J K L M N O P Q R S T U V W X Y Z

Example.	DE is to FG as ST is to [**UV**]
a.	DF is to EG as XY is to [__]
b.	AB is to CD as GI is to [__]
c.	FK is to CH as PR is to [__]
d.	UW is to VV as NR is to [__]
e.	KD is to ME as JC is to [__]
f.	XT is to WV as AZ is to [__]
g.	QZ is to TY as DV is to [__]
h.	TQ is to VO as VX is to [__]
i.	JO is to NK as FH is to [__]
j.	QD is to OE as TE is to [__]

k.	DH is to GF as WP is to [__]
l.	KB is to LX as DU is to [__]

Total: / 12

CHAPTER 10, SECTION C – LANGUAGE INFERENCE

The following short story was written by Winston Churchill towards the end of the Nineteenth Century. Use your language inference skills to make sense of the text.

IT was a little after half-past nine when the man fell overboard. The mail steamer was hurrying through the Red Sea. There was a concert on board. All the passengers were glad to break the monotony of the voyage and gathered around the piano in the companion-house. The decks were deserted. The man had been listening to the music and joining in the songs, but the room was hot and he came out to enjoy a breath of the wind, which the speedy passage of the liner created.

The man walked out onto the platform, as on to a balcony. He leaned his back against the rail and blew a puff of smoke into the air reflectively. Suddenly, the railing, which had been insecurely fastened, gave way with a snap and he fell backwards into the warm water of the sea amid a great splash.

For a moment he was physically too much astonished to think. Then he realised he must shout. He began to do this even before he rose to the surface. He achieved a hoarse, inarticulate, half-choked scream. A startled brain suggested the word, "Help!" and he bawled this out lustily and with frantic effort six or seven times without stopping.

Then he listened. "Hi! Hi! Clear the way for the Rowdy Dowdy Boys!"

The chorus floated back to him across the smooth water for the ship had already completely passed by. And as he heard the music a long stab of horror drove though his heart. The possibility that he would not be picked up dawned for the first time on his consciousness.

"Help! Help! Help!" shrieked the man, now in desperate fear.

The music from the ship drawled out fainter and fainter, the vessel was steaming fast. The dark outline of the great hull was getting blurred. The stern light dwindled.

Then he set out to swim after it with furious energy, pausing every dozen strokes to shout long wild shouts. The disturbed waters of the sea began to settle again to their rest and the widening undulations became ripples. The noise and the motion and the sounds of life and music died away.

The liner was but a single fading light on the blackness of the waters and a dark shadow against the paler sky.

At length, full realization came to the man and he stopped swimming. He was alone – abandoned. With that understanding, the brain reeled. He began to swim, only now instead of shouting he prayed – mad, incoherent prayers, the words stumbling into one another.
Suddenly a distant light seemed to flicker and brighten.

A surge of joy and hope rushed through his mind. They were going to stop - to turn the ship and come back. He stopped and stared after the light - his soul in his eyes. As he watched it, it grew gradually but steadily smaller. Then the man knew that his fate was certain. Despair awaited him, feebly splashing with his hands, he moaned in bitter misery, "I can't - I must. O God! Let me die!"
The moon, then in her third quarter, pushed out from behind the concealing clouds and shed a pale, soft glitter upon the sea. Upright in the water, fifty yards away, was a black triangular object. It was a fin. It approached him slowly. His last appeal had been heard.

Questions

1. a. Why was the man on deck? [2 marks]

Answer:_____

_____

b. Why was the man *alone* on deck? [1 mark]

Answer:_____

2. Describe how and why the man fell overboard. [2 marks]

Answer:_____

_____

3. "Then he realised he must shout." Why? [1 mark]

Answer:_____

4. Underline the correct answer. "He bawled this out lustily…" tells us that he was: [1 mark]

    a. crying like a baby

    b. shouting loudly

    c. squeaking in fear

    d. sobbing softly

5. a. What sent a "long stab of terror into his heart"? [1 mark]

Answer:_____

b. Why? [1 mark]

Answer:_____

6. a. What gave the man a surge of hope? [1 mark]

Answer:_____

b. How was this hope dashed? [1 mark]

Answer:_____

7. Underline the correct answer. "His soul in his eyes." This means that: [1 mark]

    a. He was dying and his soul was leaving his body

    b. He was staring very hard

    c. He was staring at the boat and wishing it would turn around

    d. Only his eyes were above water

8. "His last appeal had been heard."

    a. What was his last appeal? [1 mark]

Answer:_____

    b. How had it been heard? [1 mark]

Answer:_____

9. We are not told how the story ends, but we can be fairly certain what will happen next. What is likely to happen next? [1 mark]

Answer:_____

10. Write down the meaning of each of the following words from the passage. [5 marks]

    a. created

Answer:_____

    b. monotony

Answer:_____

    c. hoarse

Answer:_____

    d. surge

Answer:_____

    e. abandoned

Answer:_____

Total: / 20

My Chapter 10 Score: / 57 = _____ %

*You did it! By completing all the exercises in this book you now have a much better understanding of Mathematical and Verbal Reasoning and Inference. Importantly, you're understanding the **why** of learning, which will help you to better engage with subjects and enjoy your courses more. The critical thinking skills you've learnt here will benefit you not just in the classroom, but throughout your life, as you embark on a lifelong learning journey. Well done and good luck.*

GLOSSARY OF TERMS (ALPHABETICALLY)

Area	Area of a shape is found by multiplying the length and breadth.
Directed Numbers	The numbers which have a direction and a size are called directed numbers. Once a direction is chosen as positive (+), the opposite direction is taken as negative (-).
Factor	A factor is a whole number that divides exactly into another whole number. Pairs of numbers that multiply to give a particular number are factors. E.g. Factors of 6 are 1 and 6, 2 and 3.
Highest Common Factor	When looking at 2 or more numbers, they may all have a common factor, but the Highest Common Factor (HCF) is the largest of these common factors.
Inference	A conclusion reached on the basis of evidence and reasoning and looking beyond what is stated in the text and finding the ideas to which the author only hints. In this book we're looking specifically at language inference.
Integer	A number with no fractional part and no decimals. These can be negative numbers.
Lowest Common Multiple	The LCM of 2 or more numbers is the smallest number than can be divided by them without leaving a remainder.
Mathematical Reasoning	Reasoning in Mathematics is the process of applying logical and critical thinking to a Mathematical problem in order to work out the correct strategy to use (and as importantly, not to use) in reaching a solution.
Mean	Mean is the total of all the numbers divided by the number of items.
Median	Median is the middle number when all of the numbers are arranged from smallest to largest.
Mode	Mode is the number that is the most common.
Multiple	A multiple is a number which can be divided by another number without leaving a remainder.
Perimeter	Perimeter means the distance all the way around a shape. Remember the distance around a circle is called the circumference.
Prime Factor	A factor that is a prime number. If any prime numbers can be multiplied to give the original number then we say that this number is a prime factor. Example: The prime factors of 15 are 3 and 5 (because $3 \times 5 - 15$, and 3 and 5 are prime numbers).
Prime Factorisation	Prime factorisation is finding which prime numbers multiply together to make the original number.

Prime Number	A whole number that cannot be made by multiplying two whole numbers. If we can make it by multiplying two whole numbers, it is a Composite Number. 1 is not prime and not composite.
Ratio	A ratio is the quantitative relation between two amounts showing the number of times one value contains or is contained within the other. More simply, it's a way of sharing a quantity.
Total Surface Area	Total surface area means the area of each side of a 3-D shape added together.
Verbal Reasoning	Understanding and reasoning using concepts framed in words – it aims at evaluating the ability to think constructively rather than just recognise vocabulary
Volume	Volume of a shape is found by multiplying the length, breadth and height. (This can also be found by multiplying the cross-sectional surface area by the depth or height).

LANGUAGE TECHNIQUES (ALPHABETICALLY)

Language techniques are a way of using words to compare something to something else – beyond the literal meaning. They are used for emphasis and impact!

Examples:

"A million times I have told you to clean your room!"
"She ran as fast a lightning."

LANGUAGE TECHNIQUE	MEANING	EXAMPLE
Alliteration	Where two or more words are put together with the same first letter or sound. This helps to create a sound when the words are read.	The cold, crisp, crust of clean, clear ice.
Assonance	Where words with similar vowel sounds are repeated to to create a sound.	Go slow over the road. *(repetition of the long o sound)* Try as I might, the kite did not fly. *(repetition of the long i sound)*
Colloquial language	This is language used in speech with an informal meaning.	"Chill!" "Out of this world!" "Take a rain check."
Hyperbole	Hyperbole is obvious exaggeration to make a point.	She knows everything about Maths! You are the best teacher in the entire universe. My hands are ice cold!
Idiom	An expression that cannot be understood from the meaning of its separate words, but must be learned as a whole.	Kill two birds with one stone. *(Get double results with one attempt.)* Piece of cake. *(very easy to do.)*
Metaphor	A metaphor compares one thing to another using 'is.'	Laughter **is** music for the soul. The cloud **is** a ghost.

Onomatopoeia	A word that sounds like what it means.	Bang! Crash! Crackle! Drip!
Oxymoron	When two or more words are put together which usually don't belong together.	There was a deafening silence. He was perfectly horrid. The ice cream was awfully tasty.
Pathetic fallacy	When the weather or setting matches the mood of the story.	The somber clouds darkened our mood. The bright blue skies promised a positive day ahead.
Personification	Personification gives human qualities to animals and nature.	The stars danced in the sky. The tree waved its arms in the wind. The sparrow talked to us.
Simile	A simile compares two things by using the words 'like' or 'as.'	Her eyes sparkled **like** diamonds. The classroom looked **like** a tornado had hit it. I tiptoed **as** quietly **as** a mouse.

MY PROGRESS TRACKER

CHAPTER 1

DATE COMPLETED: _____

SCORE OUT OF 58 = _____ × 100 = _____ %

WHAT I HAVE LEARNT: _____

_____

_____

_____

_____

CHAPTER 2

DATE COMPLETED: _____

SCORE OUT OF 60 = _____ × 100 = _____ %

WHAT I HAVE LEARNT: _____

_____

_____

_____

_____

CHAPTER 3

DATE COMPLETED: _____

SCORE OUT OF 54 = _____ × 100 = _____ %

WHAT I HAVE LEARNT: _____

_____

_____

_____

_____

CHAPTER 4

DATE COMPLETED: _____

SCORE OUT OF 49 = _____ × 100 = _____ %

WHAT I HAVE LEARNT: _____

_____

_____

_____

CHAPTER 5

DATE COMPLETED: _____

SCORE OUT OF 59 = _____ × 100 = _____ %

WHAT I HAVE LEARNT: _____

_____

_____

_____

CHAPTER 6

DATE COMPLETED: _____

SCORE OUT OF 59 = _____ × 100 = _____ %

WHAT I HAVE LEARNT: _____

_____

_____

_____

CHAPTER 7

DATE COMPLETED: _____

SCORE OUT OF 61 = _____ × 100 = _____ %

WHAT I HAVE LEARNT: _____

_____

_____

_____

CHAPTER 8

DATE COMPLETED

SCORE OUT OF 53 = _____ × 100 = _____ %

WHAT I HAVE LEARNT: _____

_____

_____

_____

CHAPTER 9

DATE COMPLETED: _____

SCORE OUT OF 58 = _____ × 100 = _____ %

WHAT I HAVE LEARNT: _____

_____

_____

_____

CHAPTER 10

DATE COMPLETED: _____

SCORE OUT OF 57 = _____ × 100 = _____ %

WHAT I HAVE LEARNT: _____

_____

_____

_____

Understanding and Applying: Mathematical Reasoning, Verbal Reasoning and Language Inference Answers

ANSWERS

CHAPTER 1

SECTION A – MATHEMATICAL REASONING [15 marks]

1. a. 6°C   b. 7°C   c. -1°C   d. 0°C   e. -15°C
2. a. 10°C   b. 8°C   c. 5.5°C   d. 198°C   e. 17°C
3. 50m
4. 2°C
5. a. -4   b. -8   c. -30

SECTION B – VERBAL REASONING [24 marks]

1.
a. G
b. L
c. P
d. Y
e. N
f. F
g. B
h. W
i. Y
j. R
k. L
l. B

2.
a. 9 (2 + 5 + 2)
b. 42 ((16 + 5) × 2)
c. 27 (10 × 2 + 7)
d. 24 (2 + 5 + 2)
e. 19 (4 × 2 + 11)
f. 36 (21 + 9 + 6)
g. 7 (9 − 4 + 2)
h. 19 (8 × 2 + 3)
i. 10 (11 + 8 − 9)
j. 24 (6 × 12 ÷ 3)
k. 10 (6 × 12 ÷ 3)
l. 11 (7 + 4)

SECTION C – LANGUAGE INFERENCE [19 marks]

1. It is written in capital letters to show that she is shouting. [1 mark]
2. "The pride of her heart" means that she loved her glasses very much and was very proud of them. [1 mark]
3. The old lady's spectacles are stylish spectacles that she bought for their appearance and not necessarily to help her to see better. [2 marks]
4. She punches under the bed with a broom because she thinks that the boy is hiding under there. [1 mark]

5. We know she is unsuccessful because she manages only to find the cat under the bed and not Tom. [1 mark]
6. "Resurrected" means 'brought back to life' or discovered. [1 mark]
7. The boy had been hiding in the cupboard. [1 mark]
8. He had been hiding because he had been secretly eating jam, which he wasn't allowed to do. [1 mark]
9. A "switch" is a stick that aunt Polly wants to beat Tom with. [1 mark]
10. "The peril was desperate" means that the danger was immediate and serious. He was about to be punished in the next second. [1 mark]
11. The boy escapes from his aunt by pretending he had seen something frightening behind her. [1 mark]
12. She laughs when the boy escapes. [1 mark]
13. We know that the boy has done the same thing before because she says that he has often played tricks on her like that before. [1 mark]
14. The saying means that you can't make someone learn something new when they are set in their ways and used to doing things their own way. [1 mark]
15. a. "I have never seen another boy like that before."
    b. "What is that stuff on your face?"
    c. "Forty times I've said if you don't leave the jam alone, I'll beat you!" [3 marks]
16. The punctuation tells us that the old lady is stretching the words out as she shouts it. She is saying it slowly so that he can hear her calling him. [1 mark]

ANSWERS

CHAPTER 2

SECTION A – MATHEMATICAL REASONING [15 marks]

1. 24, 36 and 48
2. 53, 59, 61 and 67 (51 is not prime because $3 \times 17 = 51$ and 57 is not prime because $3 \times 19 = 57$)
3. $2^3 \times 3^2 \times 5$
4. 2×5^4
5. 5
6. 2^2
7. a. 2^4
b. 2×3^2
c. 2^2

Working out – examples - questions 3 - 4.

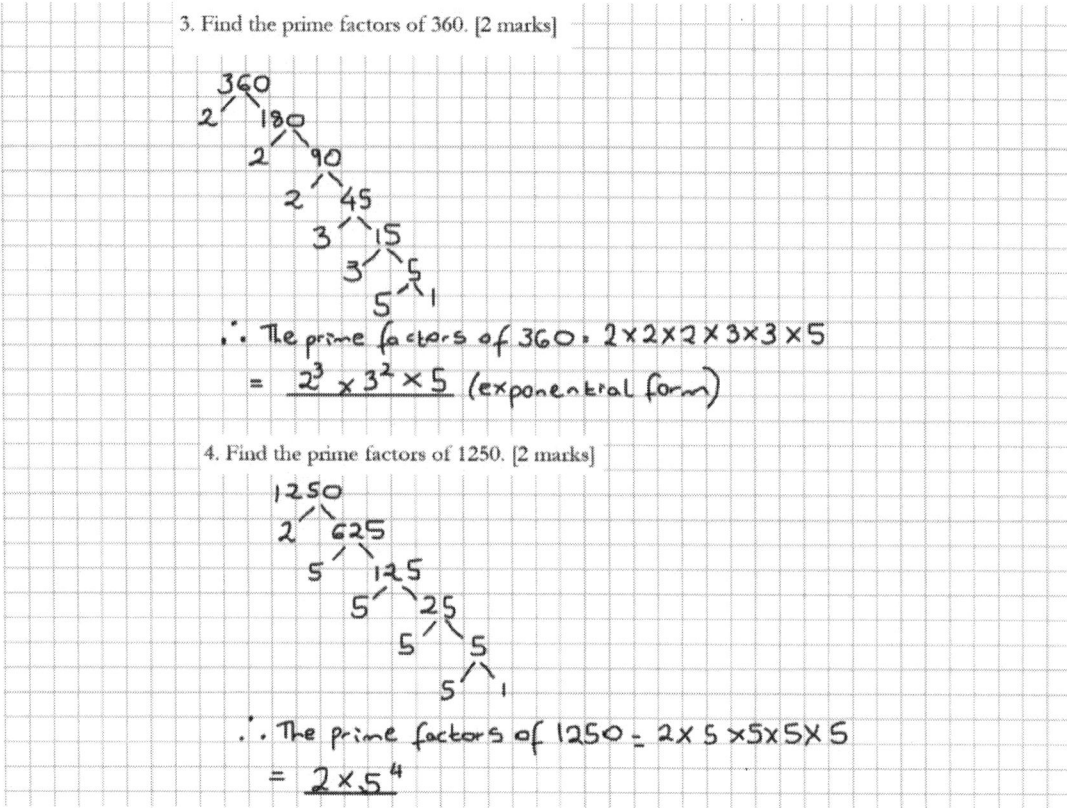

Working out – examples - question 7 a - c.

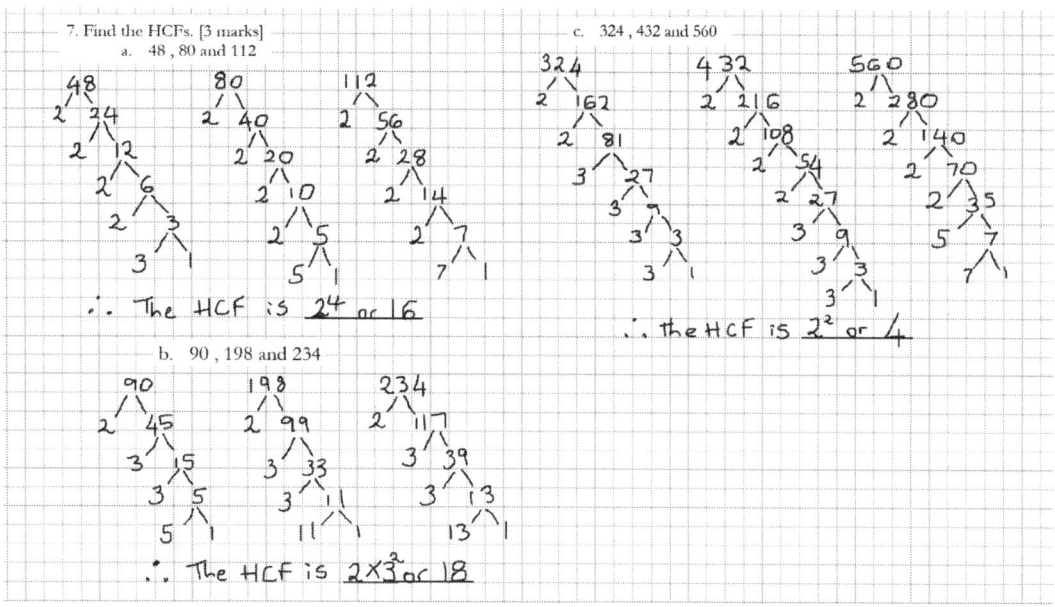

SECTION B – VERBAL REASONING [24 marks]

1.
a. cat / dog
horse, *duck* and *chicken* are farm animals, whereas *cat* and *dog* are not.
b. planet / space
Venus, *Earth* and *Mars* are planets, whereas *planet* and *space* are not.

c. cooker / eat
boil, *roast* and *fry* are ways to cook particular foods, whereas *cooker* and *eat* are not.
d. judo / swimming
cricket, *rugby* and *football* are sports that involve a ball, whereas *swimming* and *judo* don't.
e. horse / pig
lamb, *calf* and *foal* are baby animals, whereas *horse* and *pig* are not.
f. father / nephew
mother, *daughter* and *sister* are female, whereas *father* and *nephew* are male.
g. unusual / untied
unwell, *ill* and *sick* are adjectives describing health, *unusual* and *untied* are not.
h. knife / spoon
plate, *cup* and *saucer* are crockery, whereas *knife* and *spoon* are cutlery to eat with.
i. strawberry / pear
carrot, *bean* and *lettuce* are vegetables, whereas *strawberry* and *pear* are fruits.
j. actress / girl
uncle, *boy* and *master* are male, whereas *actress* and *girl* are female.
k. orange / banana
pair, *couple* and *duo* are a set of two things, whereas *orange* and *banana* are fruits.
l. mower / trimmer
grass, *bush* and *plant* are types of greenery, whereas *mower* and *trimmer* are tools to shape and cut with.

2.
a. FE
b. XU
c. LH
d. XU
e. PQ
f. HR
g. UV
h. ZX
i. BL
j. XH
k. GV
l. GW

Working out – examples - questions 2 a - l.

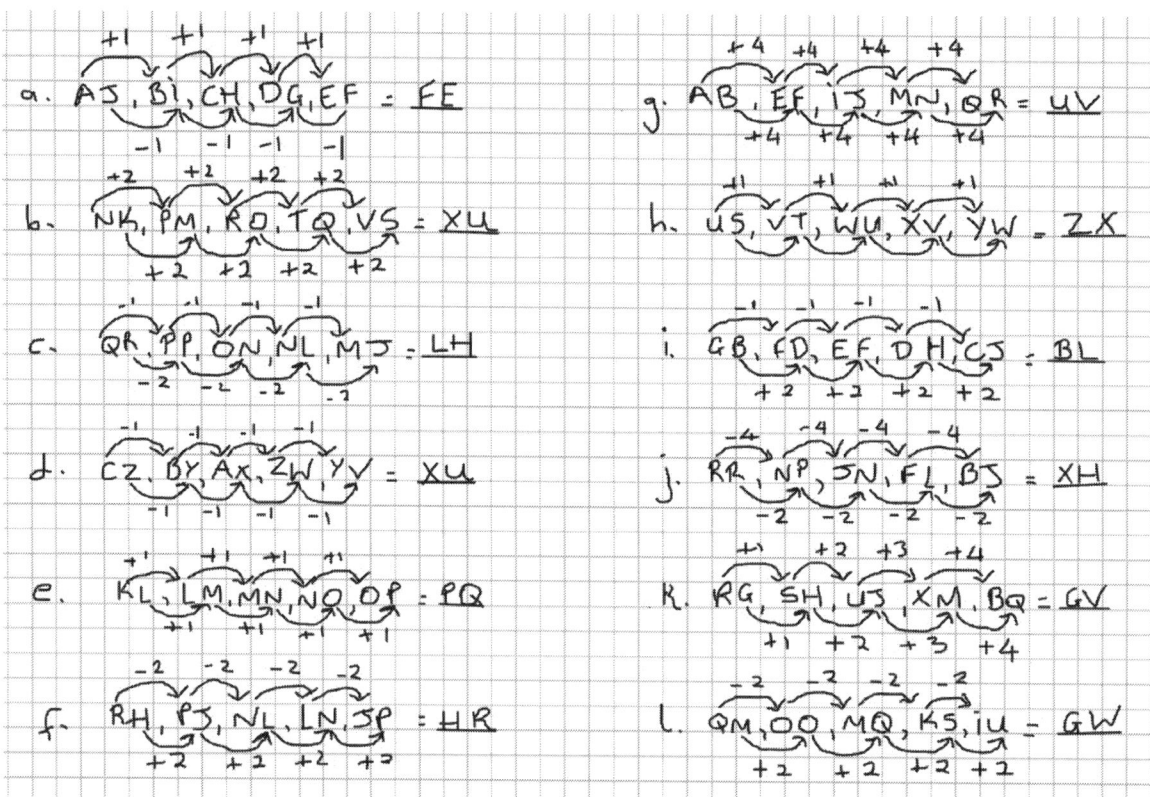

SECTION C – LANGUAGE INFERENCE [21 marks]

1. A shack is a small, rundown building used as a shelter. A shack is similar to a hut. [1 mark]
2. Tank is referring to the roof of the shack. [1 mark]
3. During the eye of the hurricane, the storm stops so it is not as dangerous. [1 mark]
4. 'Poacher'. Frank is a poacher which means that he hunts and kills animals illegally. [2 marks]
5. A "momentary lull" is a short time of calm or quiet. [1 mark]
6. "Greater natural fury" refers to the violent and wild effects of the storm. It means that the storm was going to get worse as soon as the eye of the storm had passed by. [2 marks]
7. The group found it difficult to climb up the hillside because it was slippery. There were fallen trees and shrubs and there was a lot of mud and muddy areas from mudslides. [3 marks]
8. Josh had "renewed hope" because he imagined that his father and Dr Nakamura were alive in the cave. [1 mark]
9. slippery [1 mark]
10. a. muttered
    b. fallen
    c. base
    d. anger / violence [4 marks]
11. a. feeble / weak
    b. stopped / ceased / ended
    c. hopelessly / despairingly
    d. trickled [4 marks]

Understanding and Applying: Mathematical Reasoning, Verbal Reasoning and Language Inference

ANSWERS

CHAPTER 3

SECTION A – MATHEMATICAL REASONING [10 marks]

1. a. $2 \times 2 \times 3 = 12$
   b. $2 \times 2 \times 3 \times 3 = 36$
   c. $2 \times 2 \times 2 \times 2 \times 3 \times 3 \times 5 = 720$
   d. $2 \times 2 \times 2 \times 2 \times 2 \times 3 \times 5 = 480$
   e. $2 \times 3 \times 3 \times 5 \times 5 \times 19 = 8550$
   f. $2 \times 2 \times 2 \times 2 \times 3 \times 5 \times 5 \times 7 \times 11 = 92400$
2. $2 \times 2 \times 2 \times 3 = 24g$
3. $2 \times 2 \times 2 \times 2 \times 3 \times 3 \times 5 \times 7 = £50.40$
4. $2 \times 2 \times 2 \times 3 \times 5 = 120$ marbles
5. $2 \times 2 \times 3 \times 3 = 36$

Working out – examples - questions 1a - d.

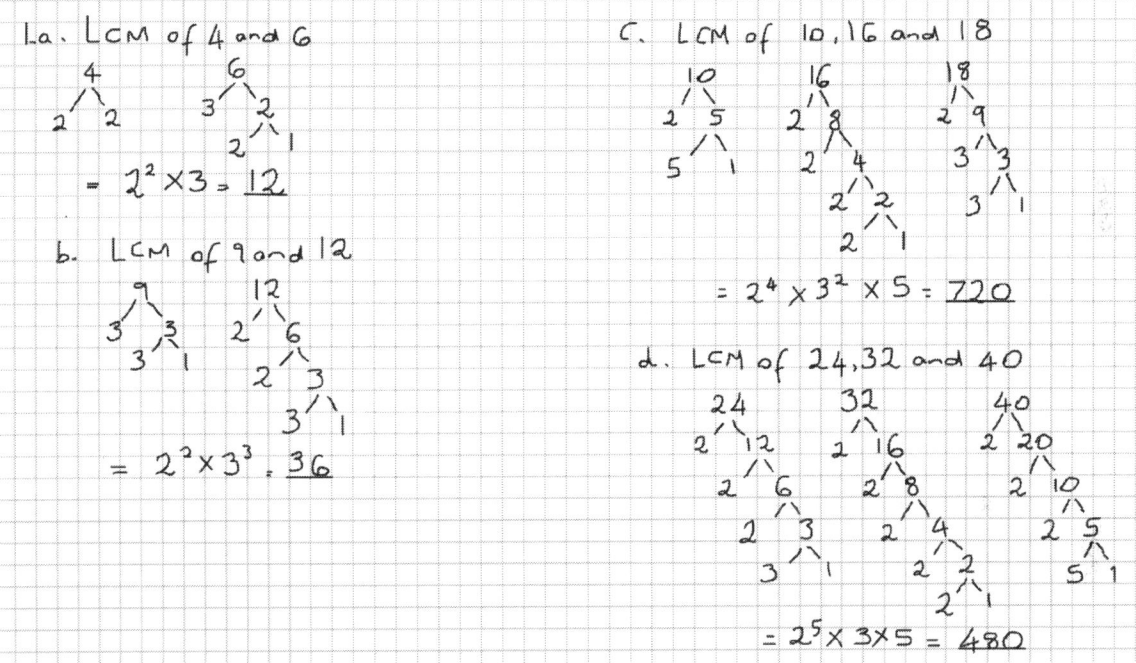

SECTION B – VERBAL REASONING [24 marks]

1.
a. TOYS
b. LOST
c. URKP
d. OVER
e. EZIE
f. BFIH
g. GIVE
h. TNLT
i. TEST
j. NONE
k. FMKA
l. QKWQ

Understanding and Applying: Mathematical Reasoning, Verbal Reasoning and Language Inference

Working out – examples - questions 1 a - l.

1.
a. CBMM -1-1-1-1 = BALL then UPZT -1-1-1-1 = TOYS
b. GHOC -1-1-1-1 = FIND then MNTS -1-1-1-1 = LOST
c. LWQR -2-2-2-2 = JUMP then URKP -2-2-2-2 = SPIN
d. 8MUL +2+2+2+2 = DOWN then MTCP +2+2+2+2 = OVER
e. IDCS +3+1+3+1 = LEFT then EZIE +3+1+3+1 = HALF
f. NLTV -1-3-1-3 = MISS then BFIH -1-3-1-3 = ACHE
g. VTCA -2-2-2-2 = TRAY then IKXG -2-2-2-2 = GIVE
h. GQZP -1-2-3-4 = FOWL then TNLT -1-2-3-4 = SLIP
i. REMP -4-4-4-4 = NAIL then XIWX -4-4-4-4 = TEST
j. GEEL -2-4-2-4 = EACH then PSPI -2-4-2-4 = NONE
k. RRLL +1+2+3+4 = STOP then FMKA +1+2+3+4 = GONE
l. TSCZ -1+1-2+2 = STAB then QKWR -1+1-2+2 = PLUS

2.
a. bottom / outside
b. green / yellow
c. herd / flock
d. some / son
e. eight / five
f. expensive / never
g. dirty / scrape
h. multiply / subtract
i. glove / sock
j. see / tired
k. fruit / veg
l. heavy / loose

SECTION C – LANGUAGE INFERENCE [20 marks]

1. a. It was a better education than his grandparents had. [1 mark]
2. The wild boys and girls brought to school with them strange swear words and sayings, odd smells, old-fashioned clothes and strange food like pies. [4 marks]
3. They didn't tell him that he was going to school, just surrounded him and carried him off to school. [1 mark]
4. I am not. I am staying at home. [1 mark]
5. a. He cries and kicks. [1 mark]
   b. His sisters threaten him that if he doesn't go to school, he will be put in a box, turned into a rabbit and chopped up on Sunday. [2 marks]
6. a. ii) simile [1 mark]
   b. It is effective because a rodeo is full of wild, galloping horses with plenty of action, just as the playground seems full of noise, dust and wild creatures to the little boy. [1 mark]
7. c. Laurie did not like the way they showed their interest in him. [1 mark]
8. a. The teacher meant that Laurie must sit there for a while. [1 mark]

b. Laurie thought she was going to give him a gift. [1 mark]
9. Laurie did not take long to settle into school life because he soon stole an apple to replace his potato which was stolen. [1 mark]
10. A word that means the same as small pieces of metal exploding is "shrapnel." [1 mark]
11. a. muddled, mixed-up.
   b. slums, shacks, shanties, huts, ruins.
   c. polite, well-mannered, generous. [3 marks]

ANSWERS

CHAPTER 4

SECTION A – MATHEMATICAL REASONING [13 marks]

1. a. Mean = 5, Median = 5, Mode = 2, Range = 7
b. Mean = 9, Median = 8, Mode = 8, Range = 13
c. Mean = 15, Median = 16, Mode = 16, Range = 11
d. Mean = 30, Median = 29, Mode = 29, Range = 11
e. Mean = 37, Median = 37, Mode = 35, Range = 7
2. 27 matches
3. a. 96g   b. 95.2g   c. 15g
4. a. (155 + 156) / 2 = 155.5cm
b. 23cm
5. $(8 + x) / 5 = 4$
   $x = 12$
6. $(100 + x) / 6 = 24$
   $x = 44$

Working out – examples - questions 1a - c.

1. a. Mean = $(2+2+5+7+9) \div 5 = 25 \div 5 = 5$
   Median = 2, 2, ⑤, 7, 9 = 5
   Mode = 2
   Range = 9 - 2 = 7

b. Mean = $(4+5+8+8+10+11+17) \div 7 = 63 \div 7 = 9$
   Median = 4, 5, 8, ⑧, 10, 11, 17 = 8
   Mode = 8
   Range = 17 - 4 = 13

c. Mean = $(10+13+13+16+16+16+21) \div 7 = 105 \div 7 = 15$
   Median = 10, 13, 13, ⑯, 16, 16, 21 = 16
   Mode = 16
   Range = 21 - 10 = 11

SECTION B – VERBAL REASONING [21 marks]

1.
a. many / lots
b. beat / hit
c. speak / talk
d. money / cash
e. slip / slide
f. rock / stone
g. jump / leap
h. cup / mug
i. spade / shovel
j. push / shove
k. chair / stool
l. pool / pond

2.
a. 3967
b. 1639
c. RATE
d. 67585
e. 3468
f. LEAN
g. 84521
h. 4712
i. FLEAS

Working out – examples - questions 2 a - c.

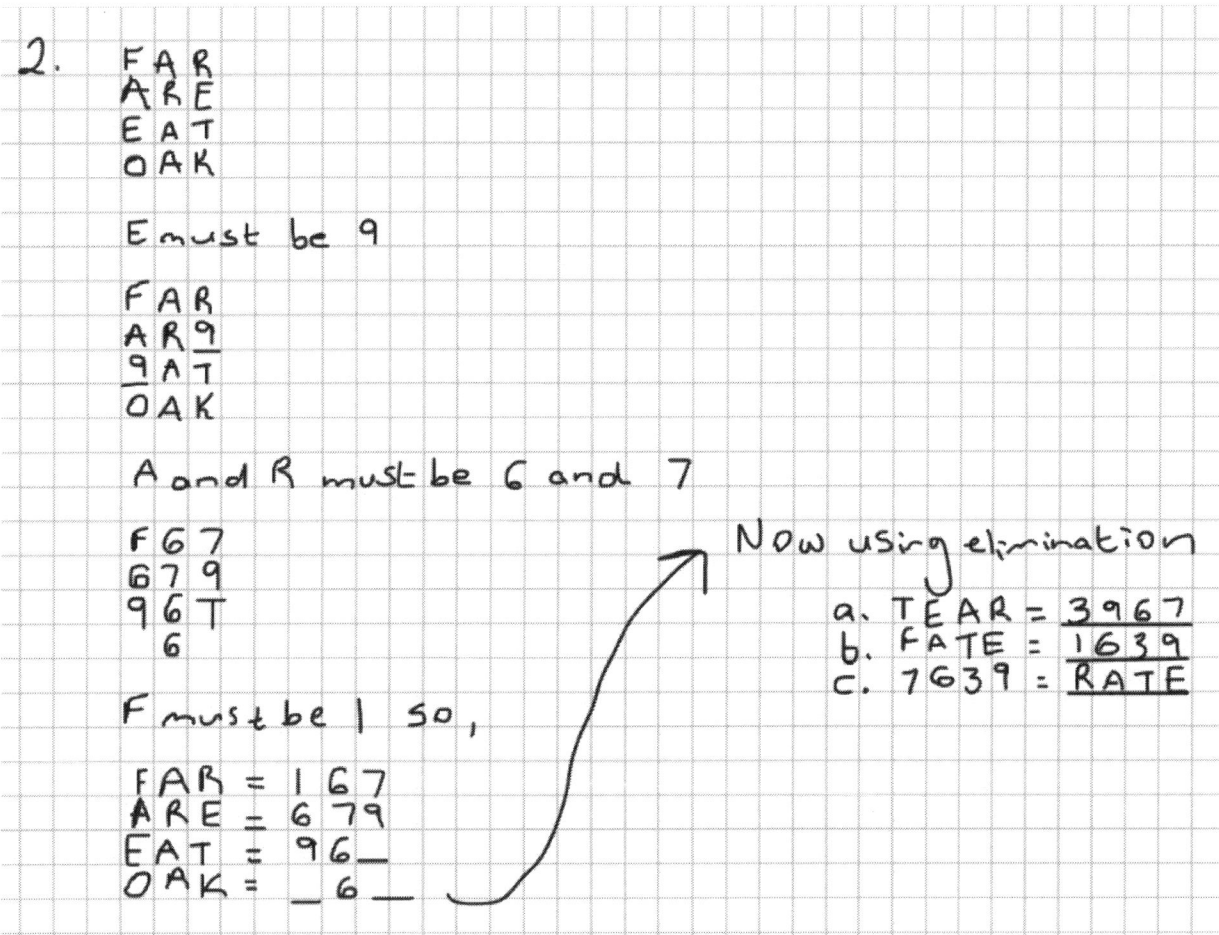

SECTION C – LANGUAGE INFERENCE [15 marks]

1. Anything growing would be killed by the effects of the volcano. [1 mark]
2. It is a simile. It is a good comparison because the falling lava is like the rush of water from a waterfall, only the lava is deadly. [2 marks]
3. A vulcanologist is someone who studies volcanoes. [1 mark]
4. a. It hindered their search for the crater because the fog kept blocking their view so that they could hardly see. [1 mark]
   b. In clear weather they would be able to see the rising smoke, so they would know where the crater is. [1 mark]
5. It was no simple volcano because it didn't rise to a point like normal volcanoes. [1 mark]
6. The fog was thickened by evil gasses and smoke. [1 mark]
7. In Dr Dan strode along boldly because he was afraid to show fear. [1 mark]
8. The noise was extremely loud. [1 mark]
9. a. dismal, sad, uninteresting
   b. shiny
   c. tired
   d. sudden
   e. cargo, goods [5 marks]

ANSWERS

CHAPTER 5

SECTION A – MATHEMATICAL REASONING [15 marks]

1. 9
2. 5
3. 130
4. 24
5. 11
6. 12
7. 12
8. 38
9. 24
10. 486
11. 10
12. -5
13. 320
14. 6
15. 0

SECTION B – VERBAL REASONING [24 marks]

1.
a. shin
b. seat
c. wasp
d. soft
e. them
f. spin
g. hand
h. pear
i. down
j. will
k. mast
l. vest

2.
a. sour
b. read
c. golf
d. mast
e. rat
f. slip
g. eat
h. gear
i. sent
j. made
k. stop
l. shaded

SECTION C – LANGUAGE INFERENCE [20 marks]

1. He wanted to show her that he was serious and that he needed to travel quickly. [1 mark]
2. The bridge was made of two logs of different shapes with a few thin boards here and there nailed across it. It was over 6 feet above the water. [2 marks]
3. c. temporary [1 mark]
4. c. swung dangerously [1 mark]
5. She wishes that it wasn't so high above the water and that the logs were closer together so that there were no gaps between them. [2 marks]
6. d. so that the bridge will not swing from side to side. [1 mark]
7. Christy is afraid of heights. [1 mark]
8. Mr Pentland advises her to do so, so that she does not slip. [1 mark]
9. Christy keeps her eyes on Mr Pentland and her valise. [1 mark]
10. Christy sees the water below her. [1 mark]
11. When she becomes dizzy, she crawls across the bridge. [1 mark]
12. kind / helpful / friendly / encouraging / supportive [2 marks]
13. a. case, bag, suitcase, luggage
    b. fast
    c. river, stream
    d. in case, for fear that
    e. bent, withered, knotty [5 marks]

ANSWERS

CHAPTER 6

SECTION A – MATHEMATICAL REASONING [15 marks]

1. 0.2
2. 0.252
3. 0.03
4. 1.3
5. 0.0040002
6. 0.2
7. 12
8. 120
9. 35
10. 0.0012
11. £269.55
12. 533.565cm^2
13. 27
14. 240.6
15. 4 games

Working out — examples - questions 11 - 15.

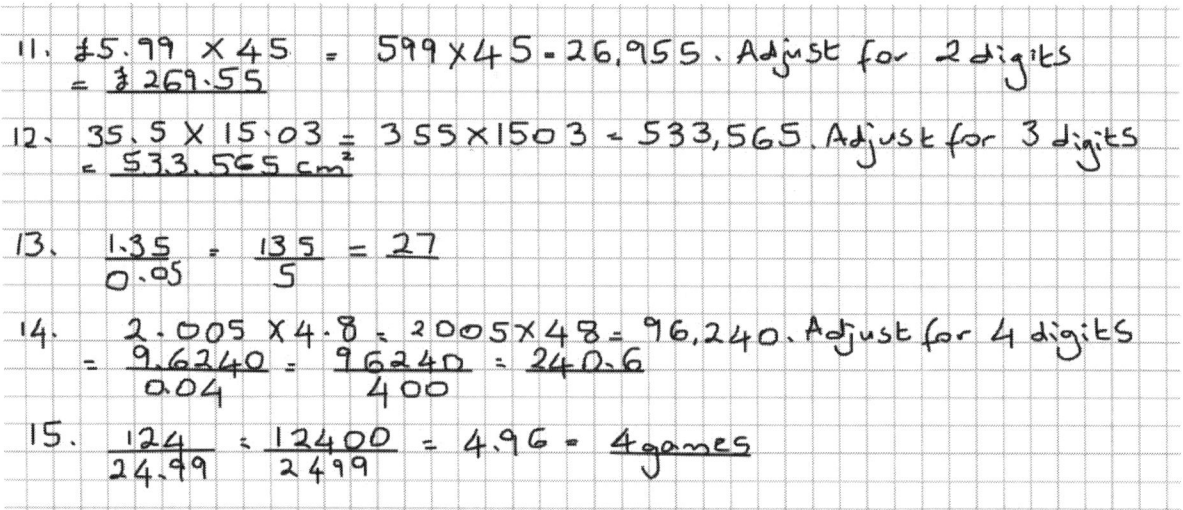

SECTION B – VERBAL REASONING [24 marks]

1.
a. AND
b. MAT
c. LET
d. KIT
e. ICE
f. ACE
g. ART
h. ILL
i. END
j. ARM
k. CAP
l. NUT

2.
a. 23
b. 43
c. 70
d. 94
e. 64
f. 89
g. 35
h. 57
i. 33
j. 11
k. 5
l. 7

Working out – examples - questions 2 a - e.

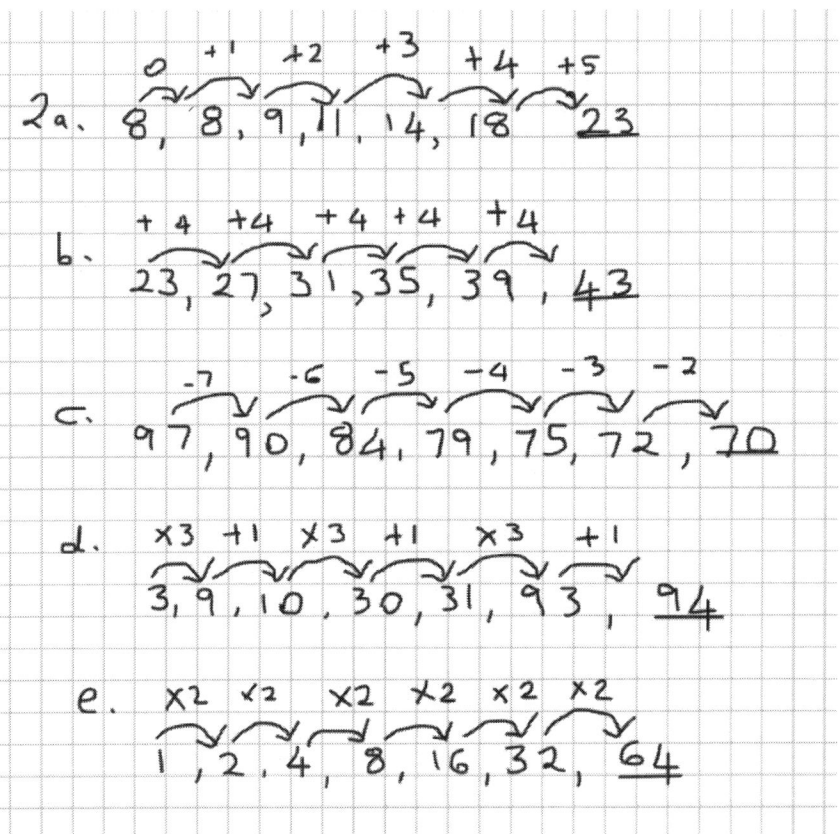

SECTION C – LANGUAGE INFERENCE [20 marks]

1. c. very large in size [1 mark]
2. He wondered what place he had come to, what kind of people lived there and what scary adventure he was starting. [3 marks]
3. He pinches himself to check whether or not he is dreaming because he thinks it's a nightmare. [2 marks]
4. The four sounds that the narrator hears are heavy footsteps, the sound of rattling chains, the clanking of the massive bolts and the key turning. [4 marks]
5. *Your own description of the man who opens the door.* The man who opens the door is a tall, old man. He is clean-shaven apart from a long white moustache. He is dressed in black from head to toe with no other colour. He speaks with an unusual accent, although he uses superb English. [4 marks]
6. a. in a polite manner. [1 mark]
7. His handshake is too firm and tight and makes the narrator flinch. The man's hands are also as cold as ice.[2 marks]
8. a worthy of notice
   b. gaps, spaces, cracks
   c. serious [3 marks]

ANSWERS

CHAPTER 7

SECTION A – MATHEMATICAL REASONING [15 marks]

1. a. $3/20$ b. $3/5$ c. $7/20$ d. $3/25$ e. $3/2$ or $1\,1/2$
2. a. 10% b. 16% c. 84.5% d. 100% e. 172%
3. 150 male
4. 33
5. 43%
6. 6
7. 36%

Working out – examples - questions 1 - 2.

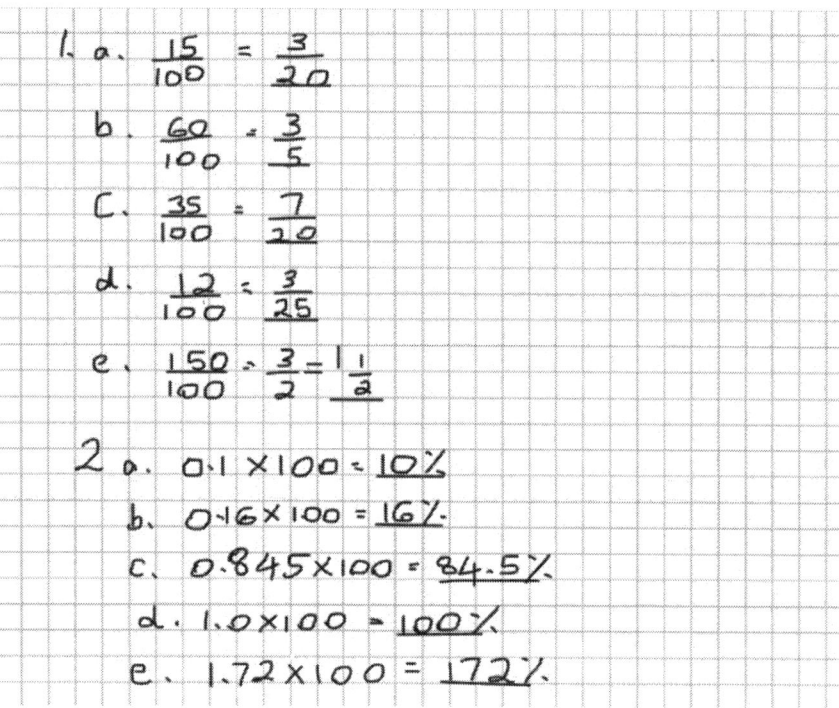

SECTION B – VERBAL REASONING [24 marks]

1.
a. E
b. A
c. B
d. A
e. E
f. A
g. A
h. E
i. B
j. A
k. A
l. E

2.
a. thin king
b. no thing
c. pea nut
d. beg in
e. not ice
f. direct or
g. week end
h. bed room
i. with out
j. under stand
k. import ant
l. so wing

Working out – examples - questions 1 a – l.

1a. 2 + 4 + 6 = 12 = E
b. 6 + 9 − 12 = 3 = A
c. 4 + 5 + 6 − 10 = 5 = B
d. 7 + 10 − 11 = 6 = A
e. 22 − 4 − 5 = 13 = E
f. 12 + 5 − 7 = 10 = A
g. 14 + 6 + 8 − 12 = 16 = A
h. 9 + 16 − 6 = 19 = E
i. 32 + 12 − 10 = 34 = B
j. 2 + 4 + 6 − 10 = 2 = A
k. 4 × 20 − 50 = 30 = A
l. 10 − 9 + 11 = 12 = E

SECTION C – LANGUAGE INFERENCE [22 marks]

1. The movement of the strange creature. [1 mark]

2. He jumped behind a tree to hide. [1 mark]

3. He freezes in fear and cannot move. [1 mark]

4. He would rather deal with the pirates because he knows them, rather than the strange creature who might be more dangerous than the pirates. [1 mark]

5. The stranger moved nervously / shyly. [1 mark]

6. He suddenly remembers that he has a gun. [1 mark]

7. He nervously moves forward, then backward, then falls on his knees and holds his hands out to the narrator. [2 marks]

8. d. begging for help. [1 mark]

9. a. a simile [1 mark]

10. He hasn't spoken to anyone in years. [1 mark]

11. His clothing is tattered and made up of a patchwork of ship fabrics held together with strange fastenings made of buttons, sticks and animal hide. He has a leather belt around his waist. [3 marks]

12. When a pirate is marooned, this means that the pirate is punished by being put ashore on a deserted piece of land with only a little bit of ammunition. [3 marks]

13. a. speed/ fast movement
    b. ghost/ figure that just appeared as if from nowhere
    c. hidden
    d. rough/croaky
    e. pirates/sailors [5 marks]

ANSWERS

CHAPTER 8

SECTION A – MATHEMATICAL REASONING [15 marks]

1	Length	Breadth	Perimeter of rectangle	Area of rectangle
a.	15cm	8cm	**46cm**	**120cm²**
b.	**10m**	12m	44m	**120m²**
c.	11mm	**5mm**	**32mm**	55mm²
d.	85cm	50mm	**180cm**	**425cm²**
e.	**5cm**	3m	**610cm**	1,500cm²

2	Length	Breadth	Height	Volume of cuboid
a.	15cm	10cm	4cm	**600cm³**
b.	**8cm**	50cm	1cm	400cm³
c.	5m	**12m**	12m	720m³
d.	45m	300cm	200mm	**27m³**
e.	95cm	25.5cm	12cm	**29,070cm³**

Understanding and Applying: Mathematical Reasoning, Verbal Reasoning and Language Inference

3. 40 squares
4. 132 slabs
5. 1,845cm³
6. 50m³
7. 35 cubes

Working out – examples - questions 3 - 7.

3. $18 \times 36 = 648 \text{ cm}^2$
   $4 \times 4 = 16 \text{ cm}^2$
   $648 \div 16 = 40.5 = \underline{40 \text{ squares}}$

4. $100 \times 50 = 5000 \text{ cm}^2$
   $6.6 \text{ m} = 660 \text{ cm}$
   $10 \text{ m} = 1000 \text{ cm}$
   $660 \times 1000 = 660,000 \text{ cm}^2$
   $660,000 \div 5000 = \underline{132 \text{ slabs}}$

5. Volume of a cylinder = cross-sectional area × height
   $= 82 \times 22.5$
   $= \underline{1,845 \text{ cm}^3}$

6. Volume $= (4m \times 1.25m \times 20m) \div 2 = 100 \div 2 = \underline{50 \text{ m}^3}$

7. Volume $= 15m \times 9m \times 7m = 945 \text{ m}^3$
   $3 \times 3 \times 3 = 27 \text{ m}^3$. $945 \text{ m}^3 \div 27 \text{ m}^3 = \underline{35 \text{ cubes}}$

SECTION B – VERBAL REASONING [23 marks]

1.
a. top / bottom
b. tall / short
c. live / die
d. inside / outside
e. awake / snoozing
f. few / many
g. first / last
h. unhappy / cheerful
i. new / old
j. broad / narrow
k. lower / higher
l. hard / easy

2.
a. dent
b. real

c. trap
d. rave
e. lawn
f. rule
g. path
h. read
i. tame
j. drew
k. read

SECTION C – LANGUAGE INFERENCE [25 marks]

1. They didn't wave it vigorously in case they unbalanced and fell out of the tree. [1 mark]
2. b. simile [1 mark]
3. b. it was a dangerous situation for everyone. [1 mark]
4. The bugs are also trying to get away from the water. [1 mark]
5. Celeste Libombo had to endure insects, no food and water that made her ill. [3 marks]
6. Green mambas are "particularly feared" as their bite will kill if the victim cannot get treatment. [1 mark]
7. c. a catapult. [1 mark]
8. Things could still get worse. [1 mark]
9. a. unknown / unidentified
   b. expose / show
   c. greenery / leaves / undergrowth
   d. thankful
   e. threatening [5 marks]
10. The <u>tragedy</u> is that Mozambique, one of the world's poorest <u>countries</u>, was <u>recovering</u> from the <u>effects</u> of almost 16 years of civil war following <u>independence</u> from Portugal in 1975 and is now being <u>devastated</u> by violent winds and rains. Not long ago, Maputo school children were given a project on using their <u>imagination</u> to describe a flood or a <u>cyclone</u>. When the children <u>eventually</u> return to their schools, those that have not been washed away or buried in the mud, will have sadly <u>experienced</u> the real thing. [10 marks]

ANSWERS

CHAPTER 9

SECTION A – MATHEMATICAL REASONING [15 marks]

Ratios
1. £3.60 : £2.40
2. 162g : 81g
3. 242 : 363
4. £8.40 : £4.20
5. 105 : 60 : 30
6. 17 : 200
7. 7 : 1
8. 1 : 50
9. 1 : 73
10. 1 : 6
11. 500g sugar, 700g flour, 400g butter

12. 78 marbles
13. 1 : 250,000
14. 32 $\frac{1}{2}$
15. 80minutes or 1hr 20minutes

Working out – examples - questions 1 - 15.

1. To share £6.00   3:2
   $\frac{3}{5} \times £6.00 = £3.60$
   $\frac{2}{5} \times £6.00 = £2.40$ = £3.60 : £2.40

2. To share 243g   2:1
   $\frac{2}{3} \times 243 = 162$
   $\frac{1}{3} \times 243 = 81$ =   162g : 81g

3. To share 605   2:3
   $\frac{2}{5} \times 605 = 242$
   $\frac{3}{5} \times 605 = 363$ =   242 : 363

4. To share £12.60   4:2

$\frac{4}{6} \times £12.60 = £8.40$

$\frac{2}{6} \times £12.60 = £4.20$ = £8.40 : £4.20

5. To share 195   7:4:2

$\frac{7}{13} \times 195 = 105$

$\frac{4}{13} \times 195 = 60$

$\frac{2}{13} \times 195 = 30$ = 105 : 60 : 30

6. 85g : 1Kg = 85g : 1000g = 17 : 200

7. £3.50 : 50p = 350p : 50p = 7 : 1

8. 0.1m : 500cm = 10cm : 500cm = 1 : 50
9. 5 days : 365 days = 1 : 73
10. 4 hours : 24 hours = 1 : 6
11. 5 people × 4 = 20 people
    125g × 4 = 500g sugar
    175g × 4 = 700g flour
    100 × 4 = 400g butter

12. H : C
    ×6 8 : 5 ×6
        48 : 30   48 + 30 = 78 marbles in total

13. 2cm : 5Km = 2cm : 500,000 cm
              = 1 : 250,000

14. 13cm : 3,250,000 = 32½ Km

15. 2 hours 40 mins = 160 mins   3:4:1
    $\frac{4}{8} \times 160 = 80$ minutes or 1 hour 20 minutes

SECTION B – VERBAL REASONING [24 marks]

1.
a. 2
b. 5
c. 20

d. 2
e. 20
f. 7
g. 10
h. 5
i. 7
j. 35
k. 11
l. 7

2.
a. STICK
b. HANDLE
c. COACH
d. PLOT
e. BALL
f. BOOK
g. OVER
h. SQUASH
i. FILE
j. CAN
k. BRIGHT
l. END

SECTION C – LANGUAGE INFERENCE [19 marks]

1. The Gilbertese hunt octopus in pairs so that one can act as bait and the other can kill the octopus. [2 marks]
2. This expression means to swim on the surface with their eyes and face in the water so that they can look for their prey. [1 mark]
3. One partner acts as 'human bait' by swimming in front of the cranny where the octopus is and tempting the octopus out of the cranny until it wraps its tentacles around the person. [2 marks]
4. Quarry and brute. [2 marks]
5. The partner with the octopus turns onto his back when he reaches the surface to expose the octopus' body so that his partner can easily kill it. [1 mark]
6. The author hates the octopus. [1 mark]
7. b. to uncover [1 mark]
8. b. actual [1 mark]
9. The hunters are children and they really enjoy hunting octopus. [1 mark]
10. They think he would enjoy octopus hunting because they know he likes fishing and swimming and having fun. [2 marks]
11. He was nervous/afraid/feeling cowardly. [1 mark]
12. It means to dive in. [1 mark]
13. a. caves, crevasses, nooks, cracks
    b. happily, cheerfully, excitedly
    c. sudden, instant [3 marks]

CHAPTER 10

ANSWERS

SECTION A – MATHEMATICAL REASONING [13 marks]

1. a. <u>24</u>, <u>27</u> (add 3 to each term)
   b. <u>48</u>, <u>96</u> (multiply each term by 2)
   c. <u>-24</u>, <u>-29</u> (subtract 5 from each term)
   d. <u>74</u>, <u>120</u> (add the previous 2 terms)
2. a. Multiply the previous term by 3
   b. Divide the previous term by 5
   c. Add the previous 2 terms
3. a. $4n + 4$
       Each term in the sequence is +4. Now subtract 4 from the first term: $8 - 4 = 4$. So the nth term is $4n + 4$
   b. $8n - 7$
       Each term in the sequence is +8. Now subtract 8 from the first term: $1 - 8 = -7$. So the nth term is $8n - 7$
   c. $-4n + 10$
       Each term in the sequence is -4. Now add 4 to the first term: $6 + 4 = 10$. So the nth term is $-4n + 10$
4. a. 992
       To find the nth term: each term is +10. Now subtract 10 from the first term: $2 - 10 = -8$. So the nth term is $10n - 8$.
       To find the 100th term $10(100) - 8 = 992$)
   b. 310
       To find the nth term: each term is +3. Now subtract 3 from the first term: $13 - 3 = 7$. So the nth term is $3n + 10$.
       To find the 100th term $3(100) + 10 = 310$
   c. -293
       To find the nth term: each term is -3. Now add 3 to the first term: $4 + 3 = 7$. So the nth term is $-3n + 7$.
       To find the 100th term $-3(100) + 7 = -293$

SECTION B – VERBAL REASONING [24 marks]

1.
a. PLAN / FARE
b. FAME / SLIP
c. PINT / READ
d. RAFT / CART
e BACK / TILE
f. CASH / ROWED
g. LEND / BOLD
h. SINK / BUST
i. TEAS / SPINE
j. IDEA / PLACE
k. RAFT / MEND
l. TALE / BEAST

Understanding and Applying: Mathematical Reasoning, Verbal Reasoning and Language Inference

2.
a. YZ
b. IK
c. MO
d. OQ
e. LD
f. ZB
g. GU
h. XV
i. JD
j. RF
k. ZN
l. EQ

Working out – examples - questions 2 a - l.

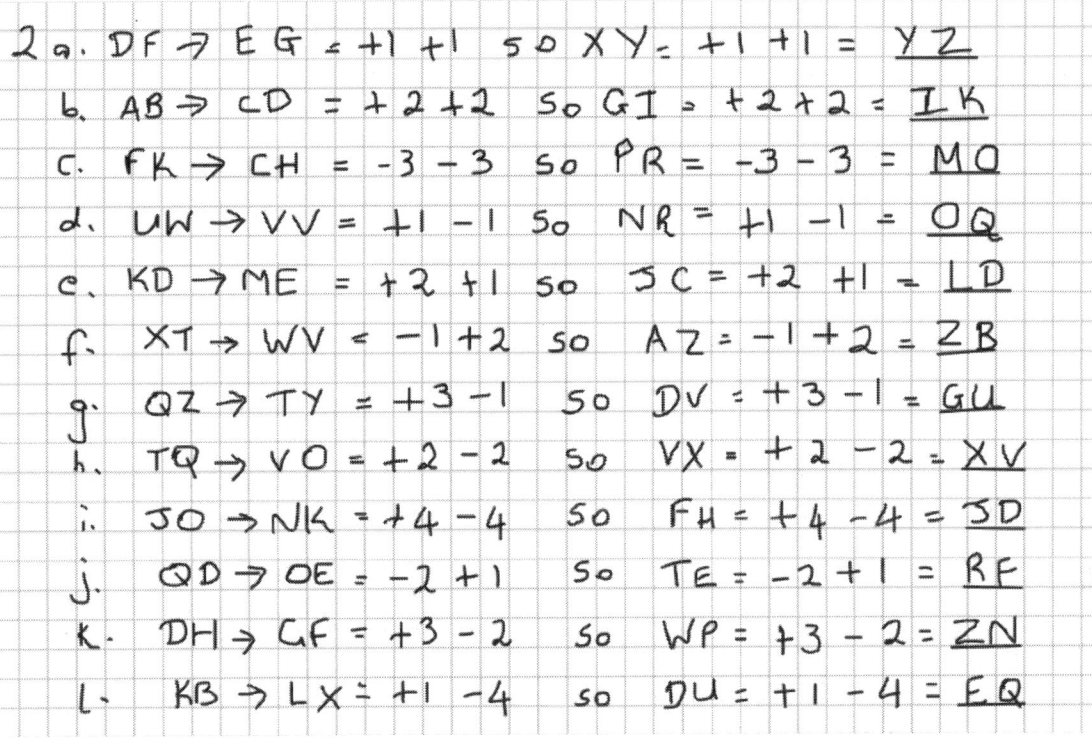

SECTION C – LANGUAGE INFERENCE [20 marks]

1. a. The man was on deck because the room was stuffy and hot and he had come out to enjoy the breeze. [2 marks]
    b. He was alone on deck because everyone else was in the companion-house around the piano. [1 mark]
2. The man leant against the insecurely fastened railing and fell backwards overboard when the railing gave way. [2 marks]
3. He realised he had to shout because he needed to alert people that he had fallen overboard. [1 mark]
4. b. shouting loudly [1 mark]
5. a. The sound of the music terrified the man. [1 mark]
    b. He realised that no-one would hear him over the sound of the music. [1 mark]

6. a. He thought the light of the ship was getting brighter as though it was coming towards him. [1 mark]
   b. The light flickered and went out so he realized that the ship was still moving away. [1 mark]
7. c. He was staring at the boat and wishing it would turn around. [1 mark]
8. a. His last appeal was to die. [1 mark]
   b. A shark's fin had appeared and this implies danger. [1 mark]
9. Students own answer. The man is unlikely to survive as he will probably be eaten by the shark. [1 mark]
10. a. made
    b. boredom
    c. rough, husky or croaky
    d. rush
    e. deserted or left behind [5 marks]

Printed in Great Britain
by Amazon